KIDSGROVE & BUTT LANE

THROUGH TIME

Tony Lancaster

AMBERLEY

First published 2016

Amberley Publishing
The Hill, Stroud, Gloucestershire, GL5 4EP
www.amberley-books.com

Copyright © Tony Lancaster, 2016

The right of Tony Lancaster to be identified as the
Author of this work has been asserted in accordance with
the Copyrights, Designs and Patents Act 1988.

ISBN 978 1 4456 5426 3 (print)
ISBN 978 1 4456 5427 0 (ebook)

British Library Cataloguing in Publication Data.
A catalogue record for this book is available from the
British Library.

Origination by Amberley Publishing.
Printed in Great Britain.

Introduction

Kidsgrove and Butt Lane are situated in the north-western corner of Staffordshire with the industrial conurbation of Stoke-on-Trent to the east and the agricultural Cheshire plain to the west. Since reorganisation of local government in 1972 the area has been part of the Borough of Newcastle under Lyme.

The overall impression today of Kidsgrove and Butt Lane would be of a largely residential area with a railway station and busy roads that provide for the commuting population. Much of the housing has clearly been built since 1945. There are pockets of industry, including the Nelson Industrial Estate, and busy shopping areas. There is no visible evidence of the early history of the area – no medieval church or ancient manor house. However, if we dig a little deeper and there is a very interesting historical picture to unfold. It was an area of small settlements and scattered farms until the late eighteenth century, then it became an important part in the industrial development of North Staffordshire.

The presence of a coal mine in the area had been noted in the seventeenth century by Dr Plot, in his *A Natural History of Staffordshire* (1686). A century later the exploitation of the coal and iron ore resources was under way in both Kidsgrove and the neighbouring village of Butt Lane. The trigger to this development was the construction of the Trent-Mersey Canal, which opened in 1777. Josiah Wedgwood and the other pottery owners were the driving force behind the canal, wanting smoother transport for their wares. James Brindley, appointed engineer for the canal, had to overcome a major obstacle in Kidsgrove – the hill at Harecastle. His solution was the Harecastle Tunnel. It was 2,488 metres long, probably the longest tunnel to date in Britain, and called 'the eighth wonder of the world' by one contemporary. Brindley died in 1772. He and John Gilbert, agent for the Duke of Bridgewater, had been quick to see how the canal could be used to take advantage of the abundant coal of the Kidsgrove area. They had worked together on the Bridgewater Canal near Manchester and developed the idea of building side tunnels from the canal into the duke's mines. Gilbert and then his son, also John, proceeded to do this in Kidsgrove. They bought up property in the area and John Gilbert Jr built Clough Hall on the site of an older hall.

It was under another family that the industrial development of the Kidsgrove area took off – the Kinnersleys – wealthy bankers and hat manufacturers from Newcastle under Lyme. They purchased Clough Hall, and it was Thomas Kinnersley (1782–1855) who became the dominant figure in Kidsgrove. He and his able agent, Robert Heath, extended the collieries and built an ironworks. Kinnersleys Clough Hall Company prospered in the mid-Victorian period, when the growth of industry and of the railways vastly increased the demand for coal and iron. Birchenwood grew into a vast industrial complex, with its collieries and ironworks. Transport improved: the Trent Mersey Canal had a second tunnel added (1827), engineered by Thomas Telford, and Kidsgrove had a station (1849) on the North Staffordshire Railway. The Potteries Loop Line was added later in 1875.

Kidsgrove took on the appearance of a middle-sized industrial town, and Butt Lane that of a mining village. As population rapidly grew, commercial areas developed along with workers' housing schools, churches and chapels, public houses, and sporting and social organisations.

Thomas Kinnersley, along with his wife, played a squire's role, financing a church, a vicarage and schools. After his death, his wife continued to play the role until her death in 1877.

The fortunes of the Clough Hall Company declined in the last quarter of the nineteenth century, especially in the depression of the 1880s. In 1887 the business was purchased by Robert Heath, son of the former agent. He closed the ironworks, shifting most of the plant to his large-scale Biddulph Valley Ironworks. However, he kept the collieries going and turned the main production of Birchenwood over to the production of coke and its by-products. This ensured a future for the site that lasted until 1973. The Clough Hall house and estate also changed hands in the 1880s. It was purchased by a consortium of Manchester businessmen with plans to turn the estate into a large public pleasure garden, 'The Paradise of the Potteries'. It opened to a great fanfare in 1890 but lasted only around ten years. Clough Hall itself was demolished in the 1920s.

The twentieth century saw increasing difficulties for the heavy industries on which the area depended, especially during the depression years of the 1930s. Coal mining in particular suffered and many pits closed. After 1945 the Nelson Industrial Estate attracted some large firms, notably English Electric, but overall jobs in manufacturing have declined in recent years. Cars have made it easier to commute to work – 78 per cent of people travelled to their place of work by car in 2011, with the average distance almost 9 miles.

A number of factors account for major changes in the appearance of the area: the end of coal mining and the final closure of Birchenwood; the demolition of many of the central streets of Kidsgrove under the council's clearance schemes of the 1960s; the electrification and rerouting of the main railway line to Stoke in the same period; and the closure of the Potteries Loop Line. Much has disappeared, but searching for the clues of the past and using old photographs, it is still possible to trace Kidsgrove and Butt Lane's history.

This book takes a journey through Kidsgrove and Butt Lane, starting with the descent down Kidsgrove Bank. This immediately takes the reader into the industrial past of Kidsgrove, the Birchenwood area. Liverpool Road is then followed into the town centre. Here the main streets are examined, with the great changes of the 1960s very apparent. An excursion is made to Dove Bank and Whitehill before returning to the centre of Kidsgrove, to the Trent and Mersey Canal, the railway and Hardingswood. A quieter route along the Avenue takes the reader to Bathpool and Clough Hall, past the Avenues and, via Cedar Avenue, to Butt Lane. The journey finishes as Liverpool Road leads back to the centre of Kidsgrove.

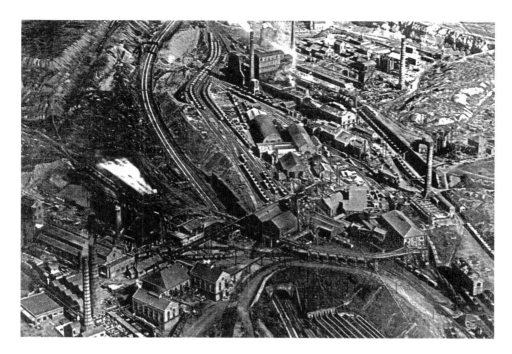

Kidsgrove Bank

Entering Kidsgrove from the direction of the Potteries in the 1920s, down Kidsgrove Bank, the area to your right comprised a sprawling industrial complex known as Birchenwood. Some idea of its scope and appearance can be gained from this striking aerial view, taken in around 1928. It shows in brief: the Loop Line in the centre and its tunnel; to its left, chemical and gas producing plant; and coal pits to the right, along with other chemical and brick works. This immense industrial site was rapidly swept away after its closure in 1973 and replaced by housing and the Birchenwood Country Park, now hidden behind the trees on the right in the recent picture.

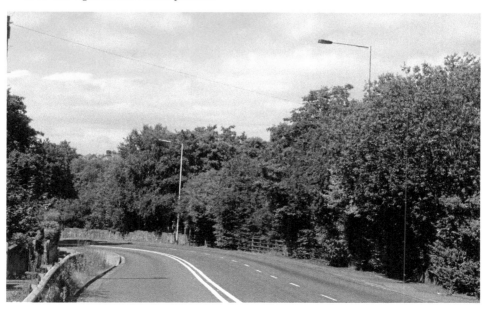

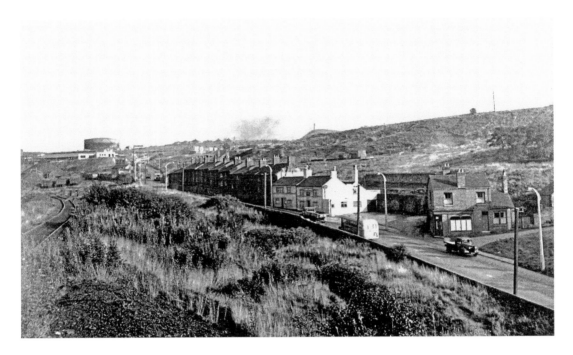

Kidsgrove Bank

The Crown & Thistle public house, the white building to the right in the old photograph, still stands but on its own. The row of cottages along Green Lane was demolished, the fate of almost all such rows of miners' cottages in the area. The old photograph shows the railway line, still clearly in use. It was connected to the Potteries Loop Line, which ran through Birchenwood. This photograph also provides a long view up Kidsgrove Bank towards Goldenhill, the most northerly settlement of the Potteries.

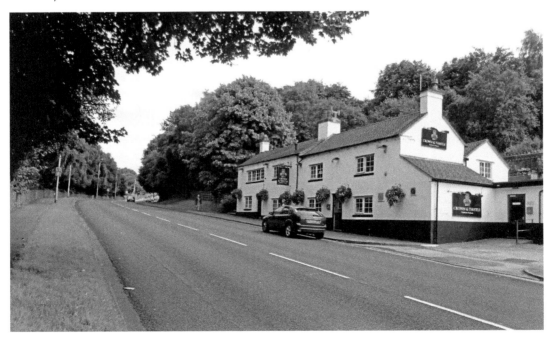

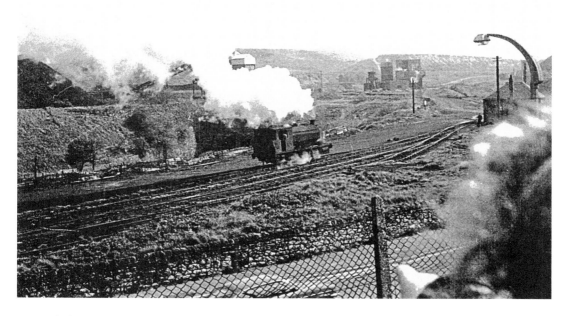

Birchenwood Railway, 1971

The view of a train still in operation in Birchenwood was taken in 1971, just two years before the site closed down, to be followed by rapid demolition. A few buildings remain in what is already becoming a desolate site. A section of track was used between 1973 and 1976 to serve Park Farm opencast coal workings. The view, from Liverpool Road, is now hidden behind trees. A path in the Birchenwood Park traces the old rail line.

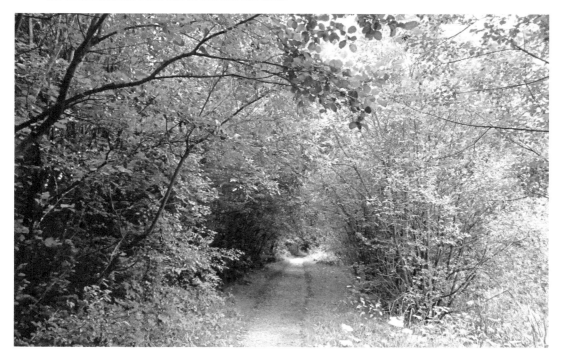

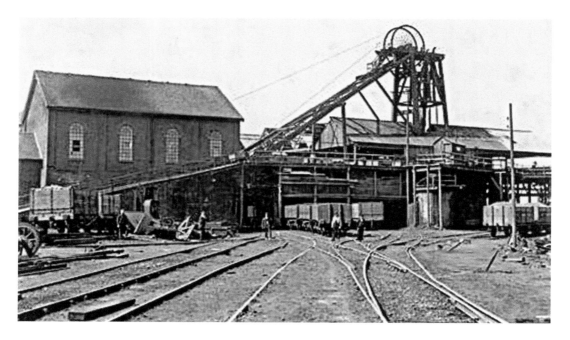

In the Birchenwood Site

The recent photograph shows the entrance to the Birchenwood site, now a Country Park. With a skateboarding area to the left and car parks to the right, the road leads to a housing development and the extensive parkland. The old picture shows one of the many industrial facilities that once made up this site. This was one of the collieries – the No. 18 Pit – one of the pits that produced the coal so vital to the Clough Hall Company in the nineteenth century and Heath's coking works in the twentieth century. The photograph shows both the headgear of the pit and some of the network of rails so important to the site.

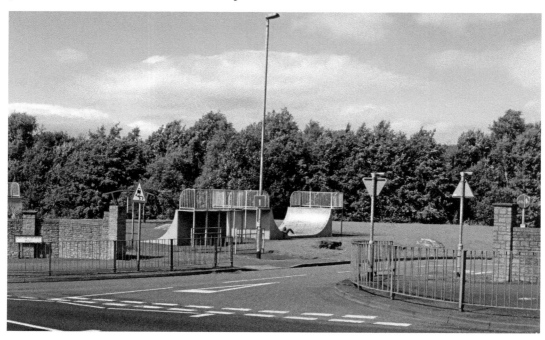

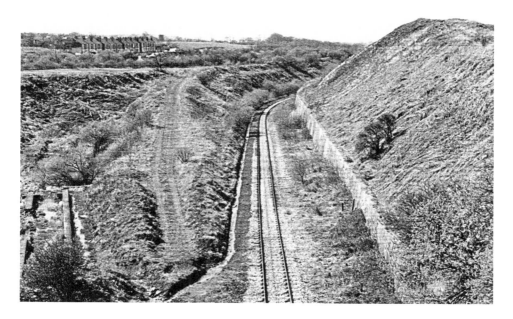

The Potteries Loop Line through Birchenwood

The photograph, taken in 1976, shows the cutting between the Loop Line Tunnel and Kidsgrove itself. By this time only one line of the original three remains. The top left shows the cottages of Green Lane and, just visible, the Crown & Thistle public house. Going off to the left from the Loop Line is one of the many Birchenwood connection lines. Both sides of the line were once part of the works, which finally closed in 1973. Now all the lines have been taken up but the Loop Line can still be followed on the footpath, as the recent photograph indicates. On the right is some of the retaining wall by the cutting but the open view of the earlier photograph is lost.

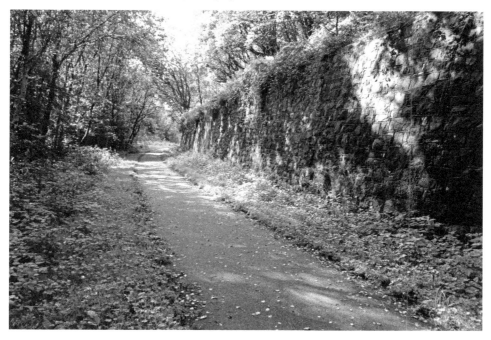

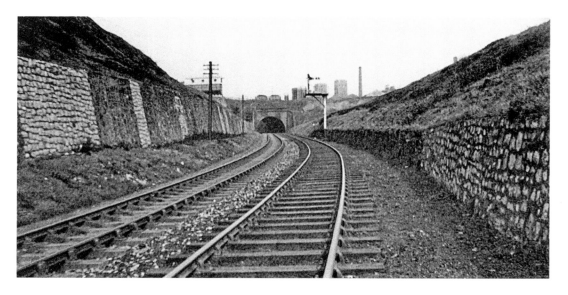

The Loop Line Tunnel

One of the few physical remains of the once busy and complex industrial Birchenwood site is the Loop Line Tunnel. When the older photograph was taken, in 1958, the background showed some of the buildings of the coking plant; there is a coke loading bunker to the left and the bunkers of the coking ovens to the right. The tunnel now emerges along the tree-lined path that follows the route of the railway. In 1958 two tracks remained of the original three that ran through Birchenwood. The line that was specifically for Birchenwood, to the right in the picture, was always called the Third Line. The view is from Kidsgrove, looking south up the incline towards Newchapel and Goldenhill. The tunnel is wide with enough room for three tracks: 'it was the only three track tunnel ever built in this country' (Allan S. Baker).

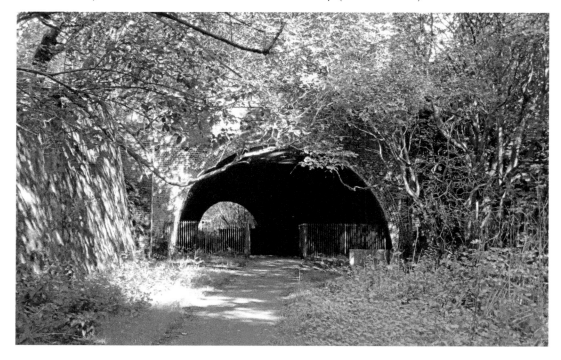

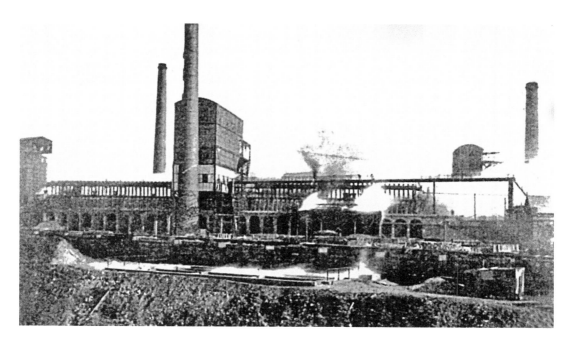

Carl Still Coke Ovens

The modern scene of parkland, mixed with housing and play areas, is in total contrast to the scene for much of the two centuries before. Large-scale industrial equipment, such as this battery of seventy-two (German-made) Carl Still coke ovens, dominated the skyline. They were erected in 1912. The large building in the middle is the coal bunker, which feeds the ovens. The reservoir, now the home of swans, is a reminder of the industries' need for a good supply of water. Some had to be pumped up all the way from Bathpool.

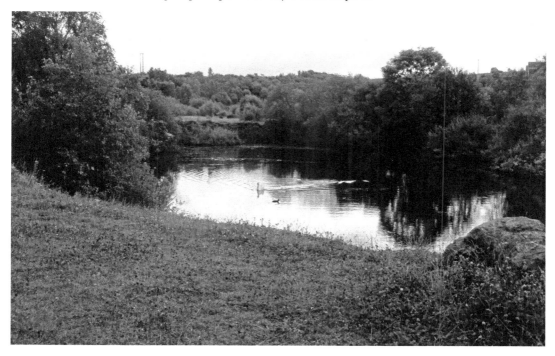

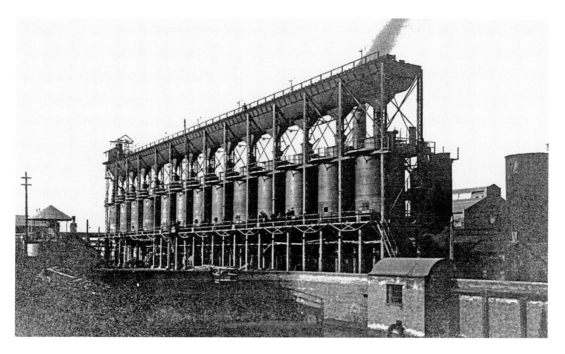

Mond Gas Producers

Another familiar sight on the skyline in the early 1900s was this row of Mond gas producers, also German produced and installed in 1910. These used the poorer quality coal to produce gas that could be used to fire boilers and drive gas engines which generated electricity. Domestic buildings have replaced industrial sites, set in the fields and trees of the park.

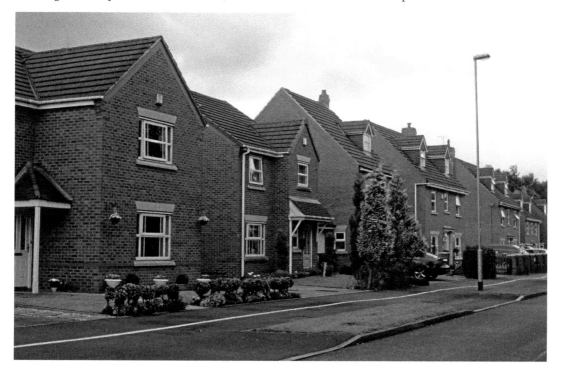

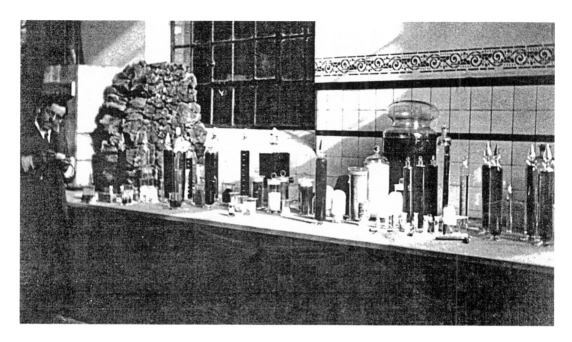

By-Products

One of the most important and lucrative areas of production at Birchenwood was in the by-products of coke. The Carl Still ovens helped produce a wide variety of such products. The photograph, taken in 1915, shows the number of by-products that could be produced from 500 weight of coal after coking. The main by-products were sulphate and chloride of ammonia, tar and benzol. From these came a range of oils and chemicals. The buildings containing these samples would have disappeared along with the more obvious industrial buildings. When the park was being prepared, an emphasis was put on the clearance of the many toxic areas. The spoil-covered landscape of the photograph, taken in the 1970s, had to be cleared.

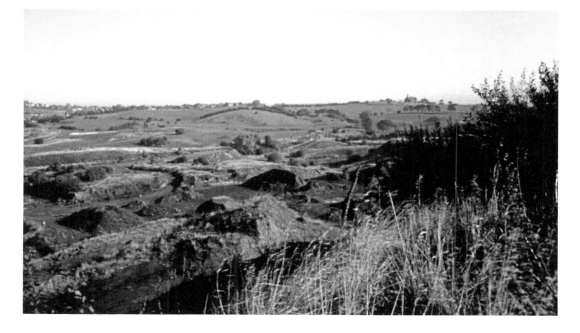

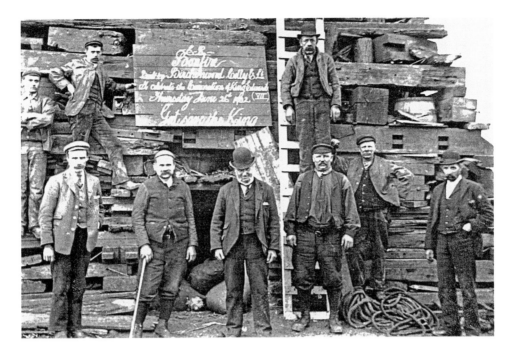

A Royal Bonfire

This photograph, from 1902, depicts an event that not might be suitable for the pleasant environment of the country park today. However, it does enable us to see some of the workforce of Birchenwood in a lighter moment. A large bonfire has been prepared to celebrate the coronation of Edward VII in 1902. The notice reads 'ER Bonfire built by Birchenwood Colliery Co. Ltd to celebrate the Coronation of King Edward VII Thursday June 26th 1902. God Save The King.'

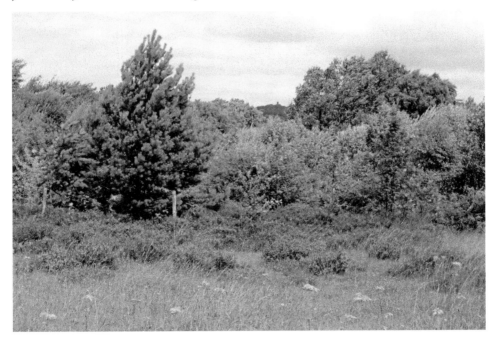

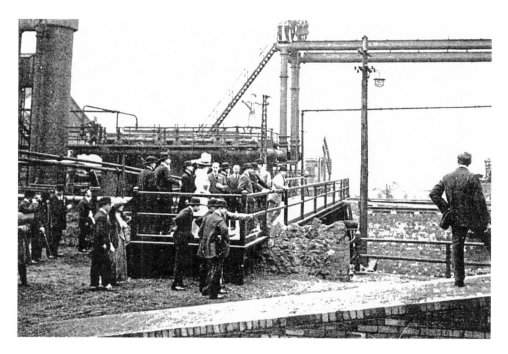

A Royal Visit

George V and Queen Mary visited Birchenwood in 1913; they are shown here amid the coke producing equipment. Explanations to the royal visitors are clearly taking place. The visit could be taken as proof that the operations at the site were considered to be amongst the most modern and efficient at that time. The plant turned all the 7,000 tons of coal from the collieries, produced every week, into coke. Most went to Heath Biddulph's ironworks – the rest into by-products. The bustle of such scenes has been replaced by peace and quiet.

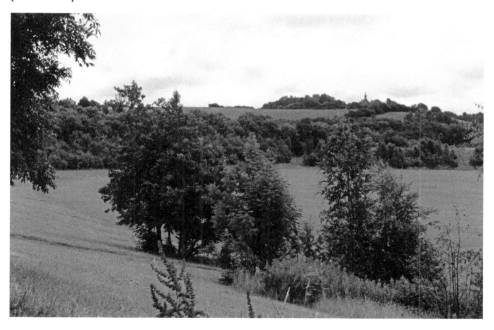

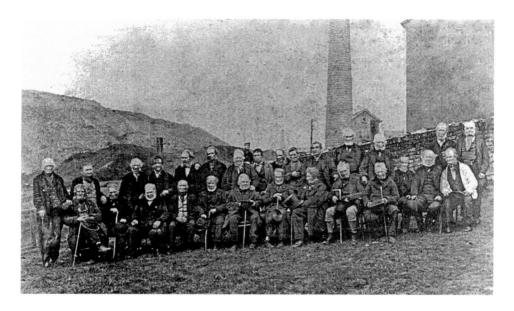

The Plough Inn

This remarkable photograph shows a group of twenty-nine workmen, formerly employed at Clough Hall Colliery and Ironworks, who had been invited to dinner at the Plough Inn by Miss Attwood, niece of the Kinnersleys. She had inherited Clough Hall in 1877. They are seated on the green outside the inn. Details found with the photograph put the average age of the workers here at seventy-one. Twenty-three of these men had worked an average of forty-one years for the Clough Hall proprietors. The Plough still stands, though it is now for sale. In the background of the old picture, now long gone, is 'the end house of Forge Row and chimney of the old Speedwell or Chain Pit'.

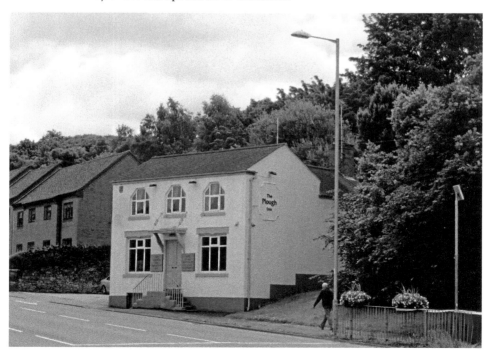

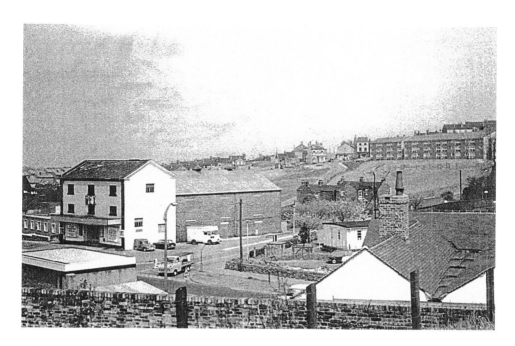

Kidsgrove's Cinema

Originally called the Valentine, or the 'Val', the cinema had become the Rex in this photograph from the 1970s, taken from above the Plough Inn. Much of the housing behind the cinema was demolished in the 1960s, leaving a large empty area surmounted by the block of flats at the top of the old photograph. Also visible is the, now isolated, Lamb Inn at the top of Heathcote Street. The cinema was soon to close and Valentine Street is now truncated and cut off from Liverpool Road, as the recent picture shows. The long view is now obscured by trees.

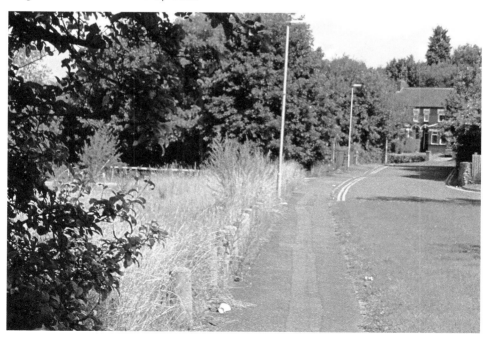

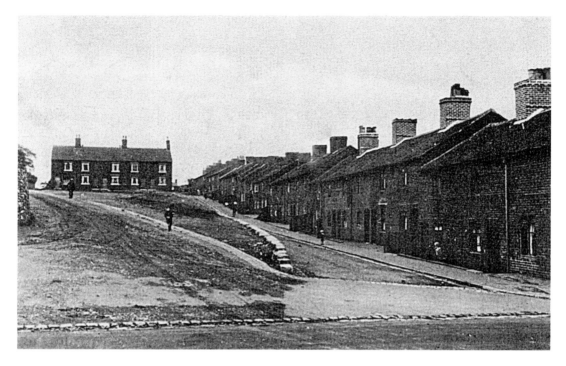

Long Row

The miners' cottages, which lined the right side of Long Row, have made way for modern bungalows for the elderly. However, the Nelson Buildings at the top of the picture have survived. Behind the wall and grass bank to the left of the recent picture is a block of modern flats.

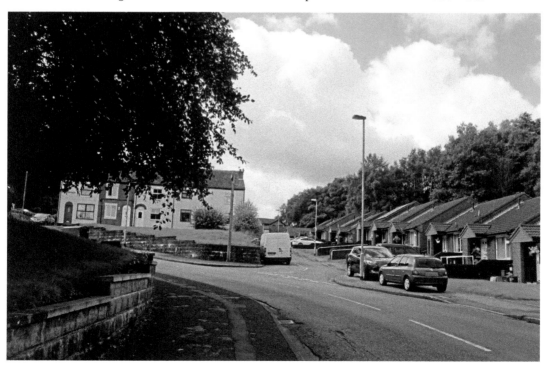

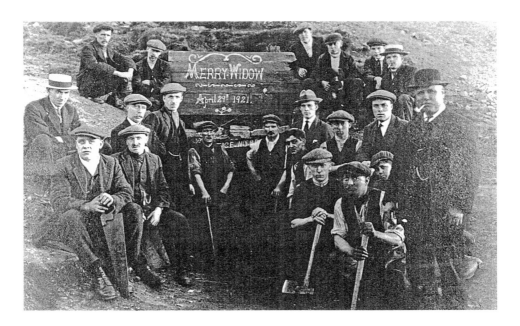

The Merry Widow Mine

The exact location of this mine is difficult to determine. Old maps show Kidsgrove dotted with mine workings, and there were shafts shown in the Ravenscliffe Road area on an OS map from 1898. There is clearly a link with the Nelson Buildings and Long Row. The joint owners of the enterprise were Mr Taddy Bailey of Long Row and Mr Albert Brooks of Nelson Buildings. The modern photograph shows the wooded area just along Ravenscliffe Road where a small-scale operation, possibly a foot rail or drift mine, might well have taken place.

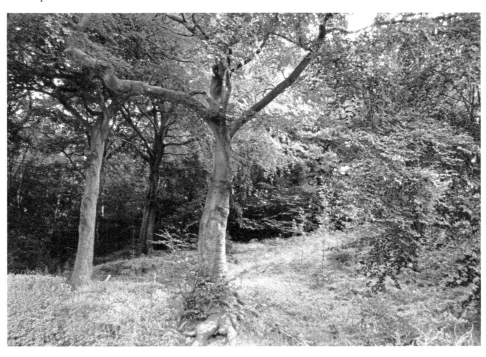

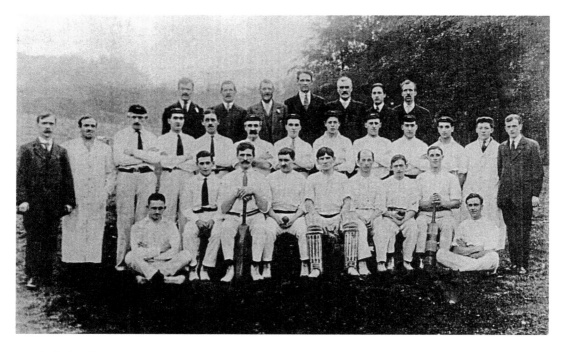

The 'Windmill'

This is the oldest structure in Kidsgrove and it is still marked on maps of the area as a windmill. It stands behind houses on Millers View, which leads off Windmill Avenue. However, examination of the building and what little evidence there is, suggests that this is not a windmill at all. It is more likely a folly – probably built by John Gilbert, the first owner of Clough Hall – rather like the nearby, more famous, landmark Mow Cop. Clough Hall Cricket Club was granted free use of the Windmill field in 1874 by Miss Kinnersley of Clough Hall. Given its size and contours it seems an unlikely site for a cricket pitch.

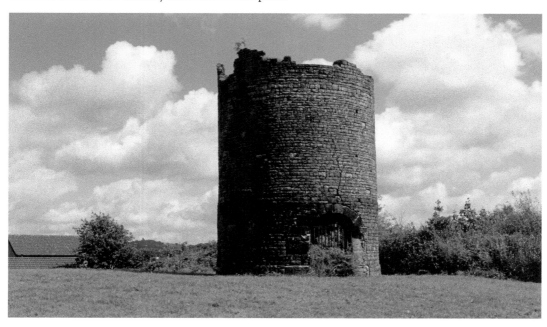

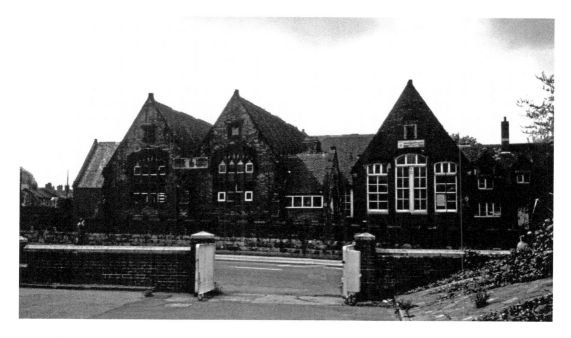

Kinnersley Memorial School, Liverpool Road

Thomas Kinnersley financed the setting up of a national (Church of England) school in 1839. Then, according to Revd Wade, 'in 1853 the original building was pulled down and on its site the present noble building was erected by Mr Kinnersley, at a cost of £1700'. This building, pictured here, housed the school until the 1980s and then, after being renamed St Thomas School, it moved to new premises in Poplar Street. The old buildings, then unused, were destroyed by fire in the 1990s.

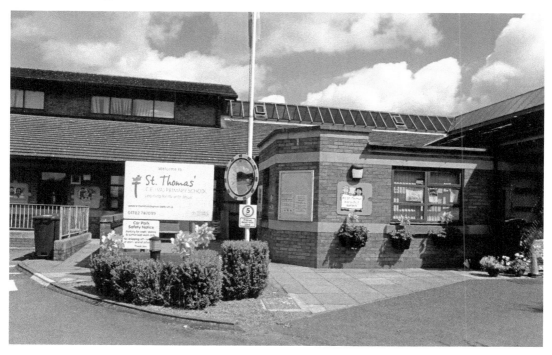

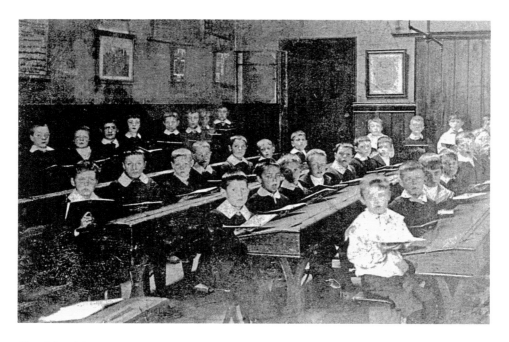

The School House

The School House, built next to the old school, has survived but it has been modernised. However, it does retain the plaque of 1853 on its frontage, which reads:

These schools were erected
by Thomas Kinnersley esquire
of Clough Hall in the county
of Staffordshire Anno Domini 1853

Boys and girls were educated separately. The old picture, dated 1908, shows a class of boys, rather startled by having their photograph taken.

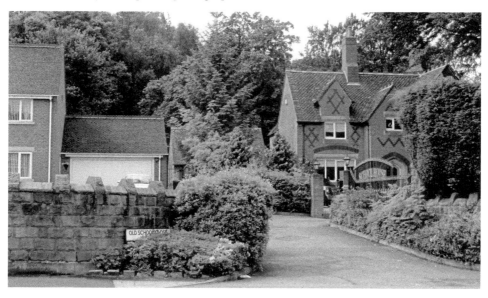

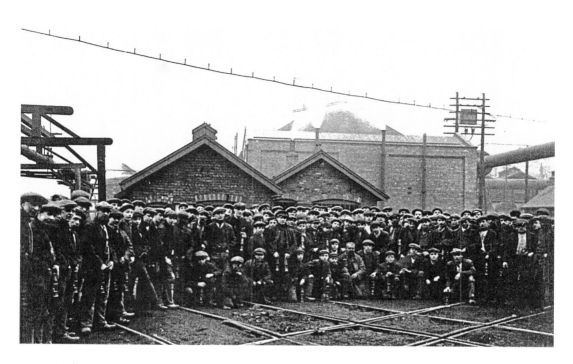

Twelve Row

Almost all the rows of miners' cottages, once a common sight in the area, have disappeared. Twelve Row is the only surviving example. Alterations to the frontages of the cottages have taken away much of the uniformity that such rows had originally. The mines have also gone, along with the large numbers of jobs they provided. The photograph of 1913, taken at Birchenwood, gives an idea of the numbers and age range of those who worked in the mines and lived in rows of cottages like Twelve Row.

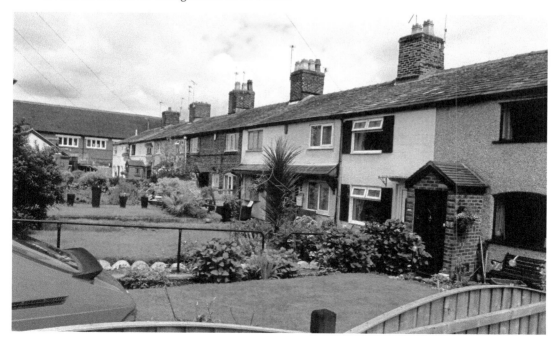

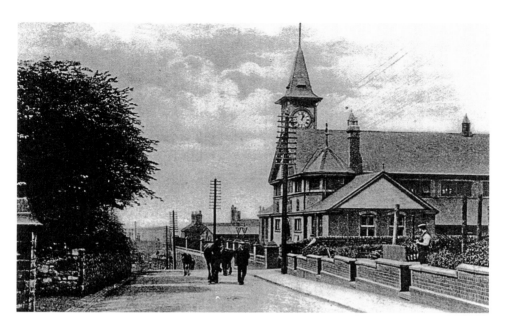

The Victoria Hall (1897), Liverpool Road

The building of the Victoria Hall marked the new local government status of Kidsgrove as an Urban District Council, gained three years earlier. Designed by A. R. Wood of Tunstall, it was 'quite a progressive building' (N. Pevsner). Wood was a noted local architect, responsible for a number of well-known public buildings in the Potteries. The new Hall contained both council offices and a public reading room. With its attractive clock tower, it remains a good example of Victorian civic pride.

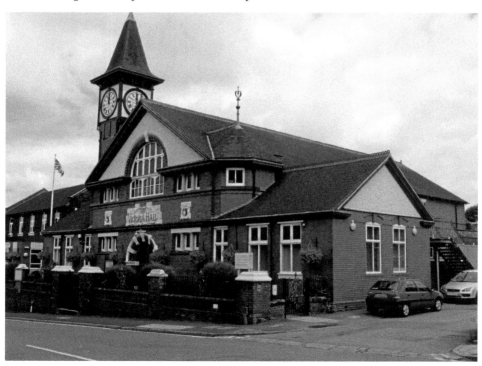

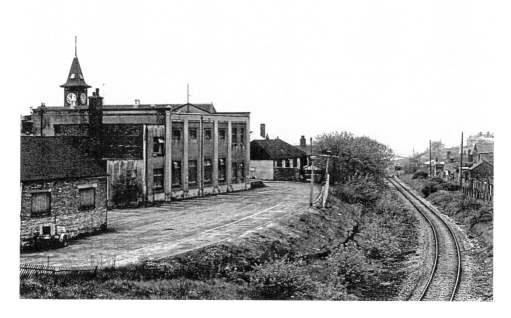

Market Street Halt

In the old photograph the clock tower of the Town Hall is shown above the Masonic Hall (built in 1923). To the right is a single track of the old Loop Line. The Market Street Halt was here, the last station before the line came to its northernmost point – the Kidsgrove Loop Line Station. The loop had proved very popular with passengers and the Halt was added in 1909. It closed in 1950 as an early casualty of a contraction in branch lines across the country.

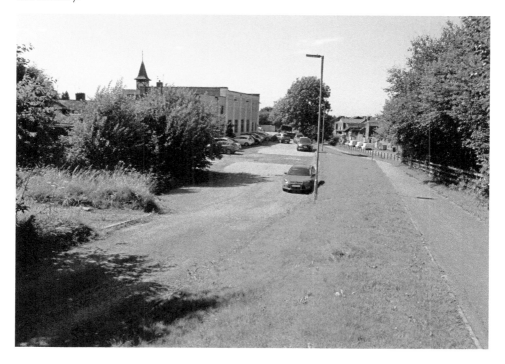

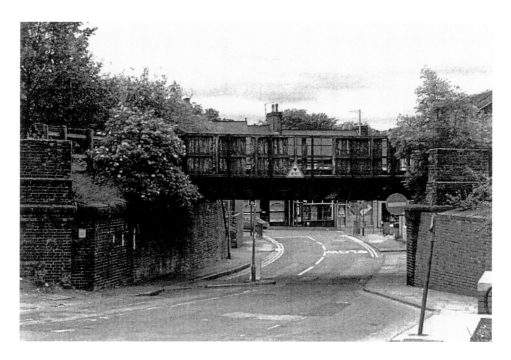

The Loop Line Bridge

The Loop Line Bridge, in the centre of Kidsgrove, straddled Heathcote Street, close to its junction with Liverpool Road. It remained a problem for tall vehicles long after the Loop Line had been closed. The older photograph, from 1996, shows the bridge, looking under it to Liverpool Road. It was taken a short time before it was demolished. Only traces of brickwork remain as reminders of a well-known feature of the town centre.

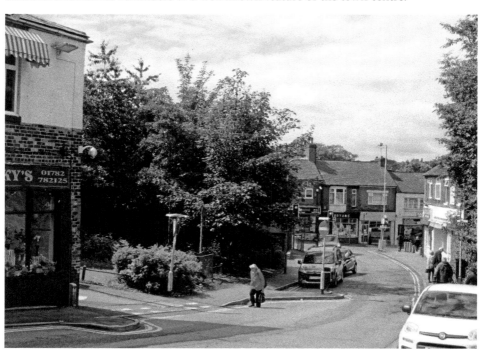

Liverpool Road at the Town Centre
Another long-standing feature of the town centre also disappeared with the demolition of the Roebuck Inn, shown here near the end of its life. It was replaced by a bank, which radically altered that corner of the junction with Heathcote Street. The other corner retains its older appearance. The former Co-op shop can be seen in both photographs. The upper floor was once occupied by the offices of Warburton and Crines, Colliery Agents, whose names remain inscribed on the first-floor windows.

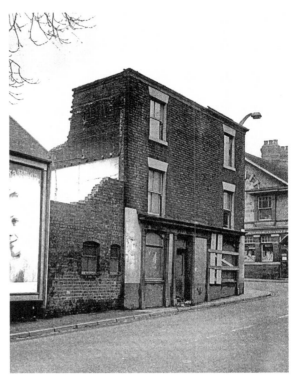

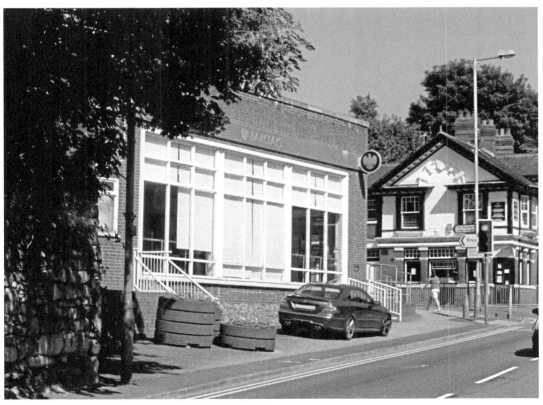

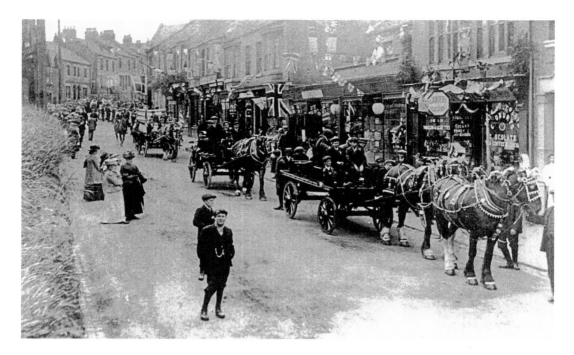

Liverpool Road

Liverpool Road retains much of its early twentieth-century appearance, as these two photographs suggest. Shop frontages have changed but a look above them shows continuity in the buildings. While the procession has brought out extra people, the streets at that time were generally full of life in older pictures like the one here: 'We forget the rich street life of those days, the clatter of horse and cart on cobbled streets; the delivery boys on their bicycles; the late opening hours and evening street traders.' (Philip Leese).

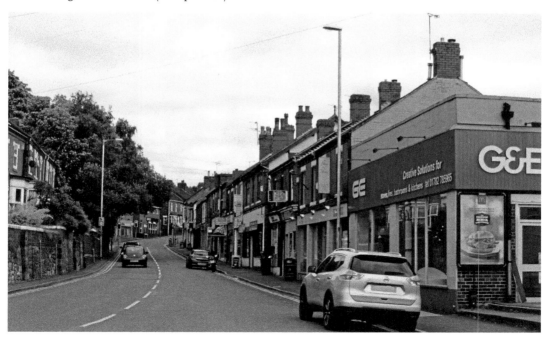

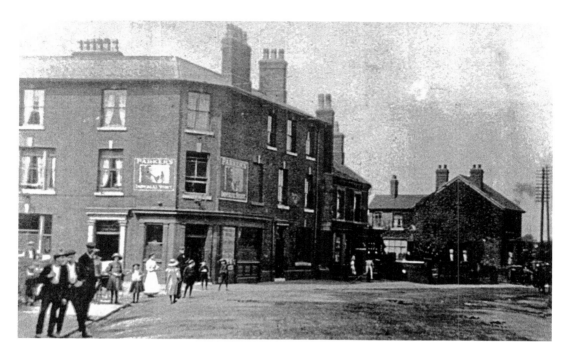

The Harecastle Hotel

A town centre hotel building that has survived, unlike the Roebuck, is the Harecastle Hotel. Externally the building has not changed radically. However it is no longer a hotel. The ground floor houses a café and the upper floor is divided into apartments. It is situated on the corner of Station Road, conveniently placed as a station hotel. The hotel was, for a time, the meeting place for the Freemasons in the 1880s – Stephen Bushbridge, then the landlord, was a mason. The masons later moved to their own premises (built in 1923), the Masonic Hall by the Victoria Hall.

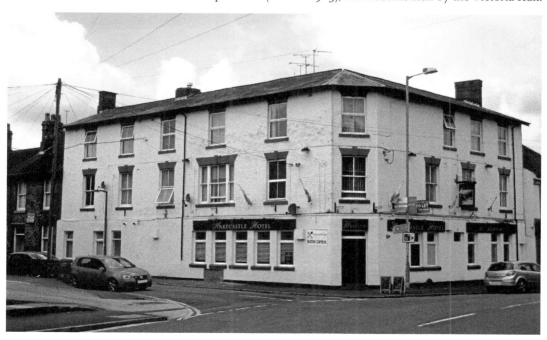

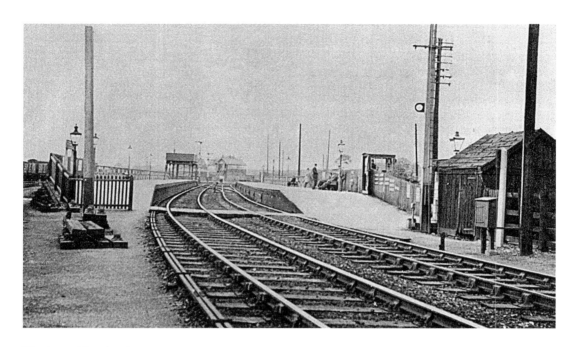

The Loop Line Station

Liverpool Road continues past the Harecastle Hotel and on the right is a large supermarket. This stands on the site of the final station on the Loop Line – rather confusingly known as Kidsgrove Station! It is pictured here in the 1930s looking towards the junction with the main line to Macclesfield where a signal box, now gone, is shown. The position of the station along Liverpool Road meant passengers had to hurry between this and the main-line station to make connections. The platform of the station was situated in what is now the store's car park.

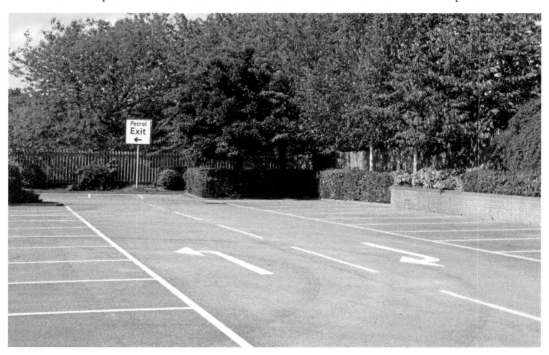

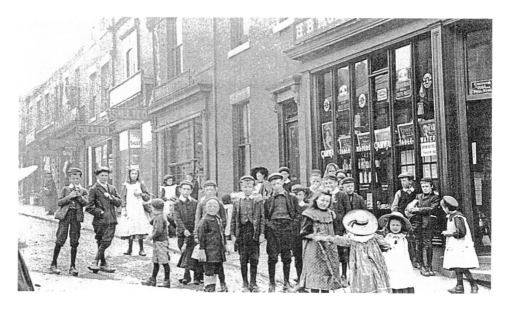

Market Street

While Liverpool Road remains built up on both sides through the centre of Kidsgrove, many other town centre streets have seen considerable demolition or, in some cases, have disappeared altogether. The lower side of Market Street has survived and retains its mixture of shops, a pub and restaurants. The buildings, at least above their shop frontages, are little changed. The other side of the street has changed out of all recognition. Today a store and its car park have replaced a row of shops.

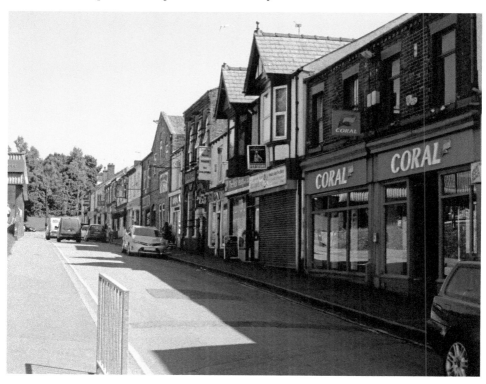

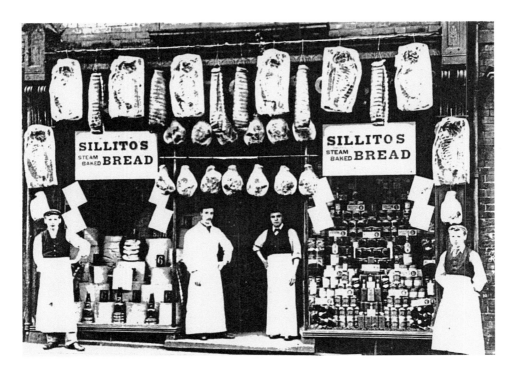

Sillito's

Sillito's was an older shop, listed in Kelly's Directories of 1892 and 1912 as a grocers at No. 4 Market Street. It was clearly another well-stocked shop, selling a variety of foodstuffs. It is shown too in the earlier view of Market Street. The changed frontage and type of business is apparent in the recent picture.

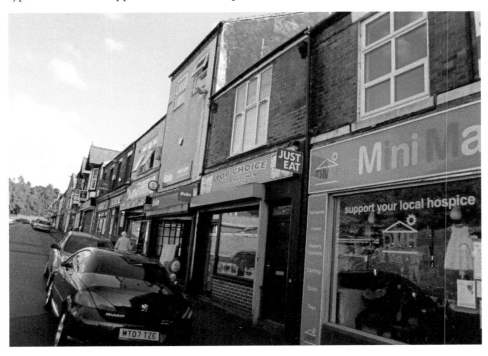

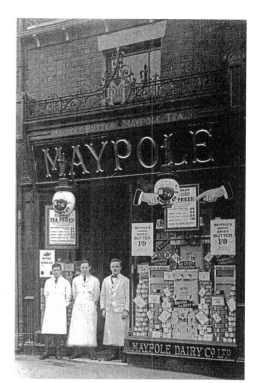

The Maypole

Fortunately a number of photographs of shop exteriors have survived, in this case it is the Maypole at No. 20 Market Street. Maypole Dairy Co. Ltd was founded as a family provisions business in Wolverhampton by George Watson in 1887. It grew into a chain and its thousandth shop opened in 1926. Today's shop, with its altered frontage, is occupied by a local business that still sells food products.

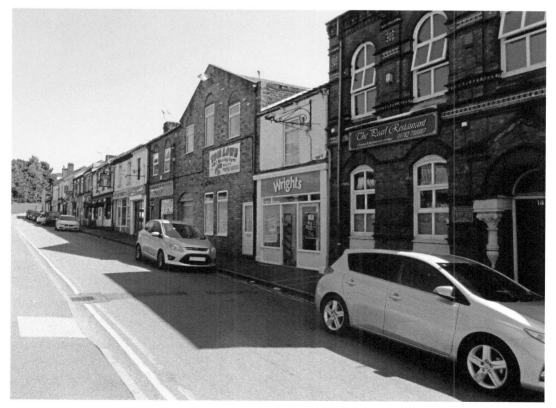

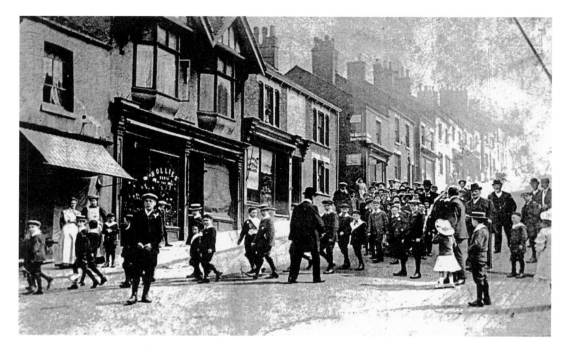

Heathcote Street

The early twentieth-century photograph, looking up Heathcote Street, illustrates quite dramatically the changing street scene when compared to that of the present day. Here children are being shepherded along, adding to the busy appearance of the street. It is now usual to see a few pedestrians, mostly on their way to their cars. These large open spaces were once the homes and workplaces of many Kidsgrove families.

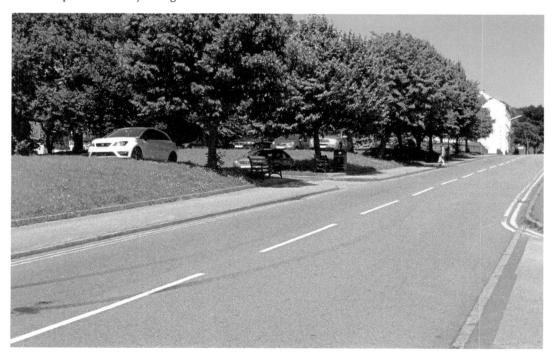

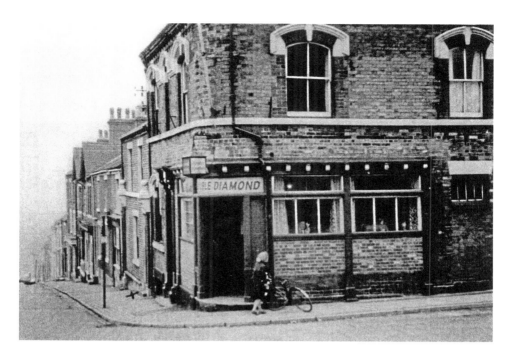

The Lamb Hotel

At the top of Heathcote Street, at its junction with Lamb Street, was the Lamb Hotel. The old photograph, probably from the 1950s, was taken before the demolition of most of Heathcote Street. It now stands forlornly, no longer occupied but retaining its ceramic lamb plaque at the top of the corner gable. The Lamb and an empty building opposite are all that remain of a once busy street.

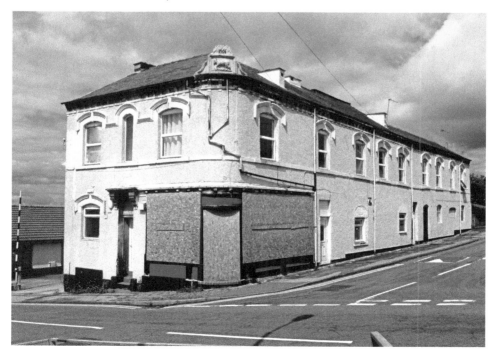

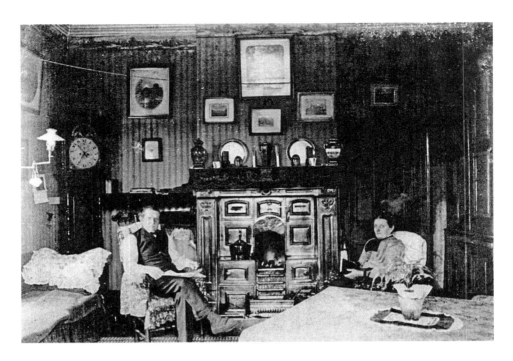

Queen Street

While a number of houses have been demolished in Queen Street, it still has the appearance of an older Kidsgrove before the widespread demolitions of the 1960s. The interior of these houses will have also changed drastically from that shown in the wonderfully detailed (undated) old photograph taken inside a Queen Street house.

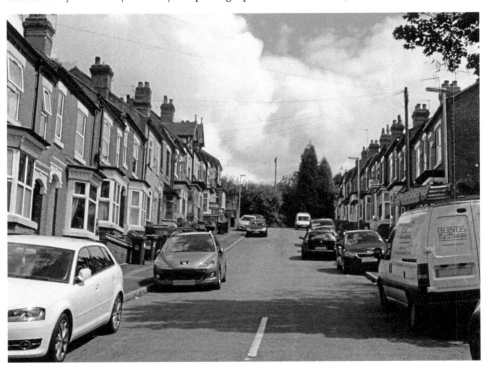

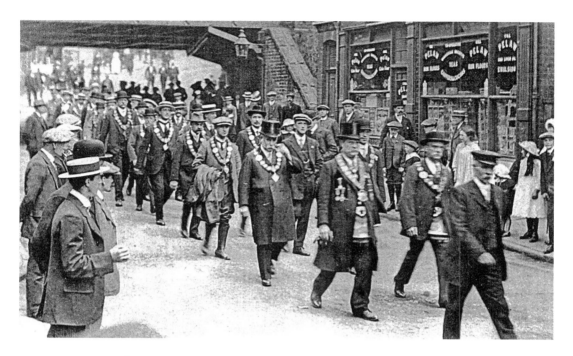

A Procession from Heathcote Street

This stately procession, emerging from under the Loop Line Bridge onto Liverpool Road, was organised by the Royal Antediluvian Order of Buffaloes. The Buffaloes, like the Oddfellows and Foresters, was a friendly society that had been set up in the nineteenth century. Through insurance and other schemes they provided benefits in the event of sickness, accident or death in an age before government welfare schemes, which were just emerging around the time this photograph was taken.

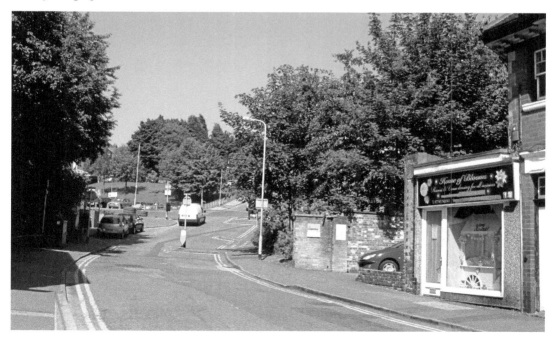

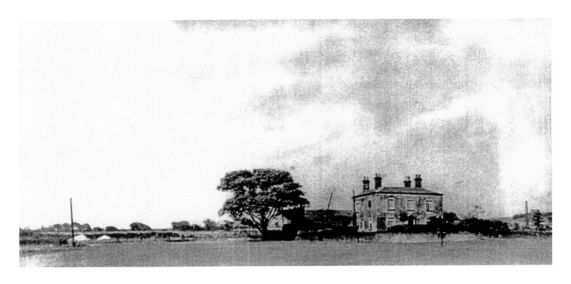

Whitehall

Whitehall Avenue, lined with modern houses, seems an unlikely site for a once grand hall. Whitehall, shown in the old photograph, was the house built by John Gilbert the younger, son of the John Gilbert who worked with James Brindley on the building of the Trent and Mersey Canal. The Gilberts had prospered as a result of their work on the canal, acquiring interests in the Kidsgrove collieries and buying land. Later Gilbert decided Whitehall was not big enough or impressive enough for a man of substance and built Clough Hall. Whitehall later became a farm but the house was demolished in the 1950s. The present building, on the approximate site of the hall, is the Whitehall Avenue Community Centre.

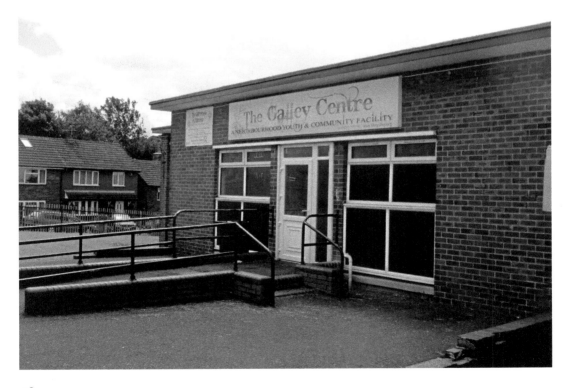

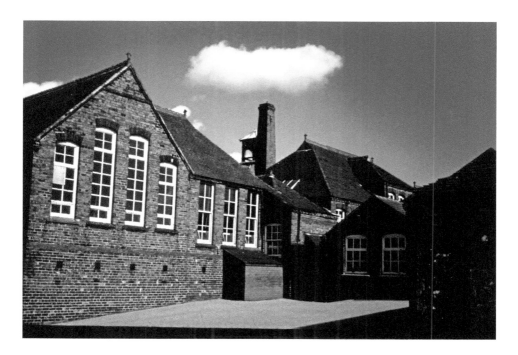

Dove Bank School

The building of Dove Bank School in 1879 marked an important advance in education in the Kidsgrove area. It was the first board school to be set up in Kidsgrove under the 1870 Education Act. Before that the majority of schools were either Church of England national schools or Nonconformist schools. By 1880, education up to the age of ten was compulsory and by 1891 it was free. The old picture shows the board school building. This was demolished in the 1960s and replaced by the present buildings of Dove Bank Primary School.

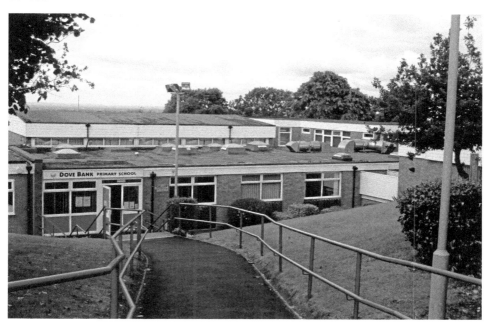

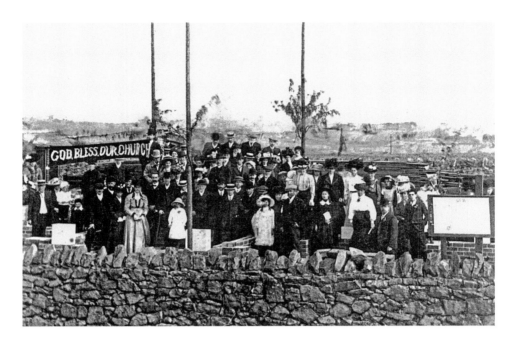

Whitehill Methodist Community Church

Built in 1912, this Primitive Methodist church was known as the 'top' chapel as opposed to the 'bottom' chapel, Whitehill Wesleyan Chapel. This was situated lower down on Whitehill Road but later demolished. The old photograph shows the ceremony of laying the foundation stone of the chapel. The notice to the right reads 'New Primitive Methodist Church.' Primitive Methodism was strong in mining areas, where it was a rival to Wesleyan Methodism. Kidsgrove was close to Mow Cop where the Primitive movement began under the leadership of Hugh Bourne and William Clowes. Whitehill has grown into a large residential area and a community centre has been built onto the chapel.

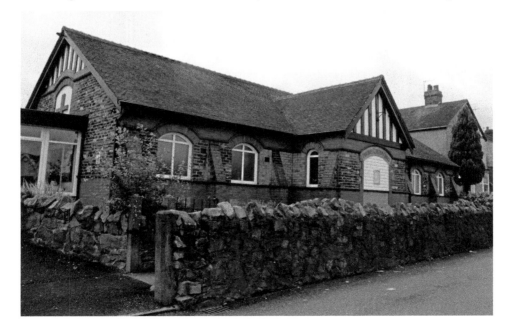

Harecastle Tunnel, the Trent and Mersey Canal

A short distance from Liverpool Road a path leads down to where the development of Kidsgrove as an industrial town could be said to have begun – the Harecastle Tunnel built between 1776 and 1787. The Trent and Mersey Canal, wanted by Josiah Wedgwood and his fellow Pottery owners, was engineered by James Brindley. When construction reached the Kidsgrove area, Brindley had to overcome the problem of a hill that stood in his way. The Harecastle Tunnel was his answer. The entrance to his tunnel is shown in both photographs. In the old photograph, the lock-keeper's cottage is shown above the tunnel entrance. It has since been demolished and the lock-keeper's office is by the canal.

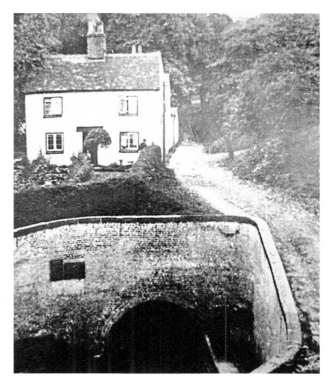

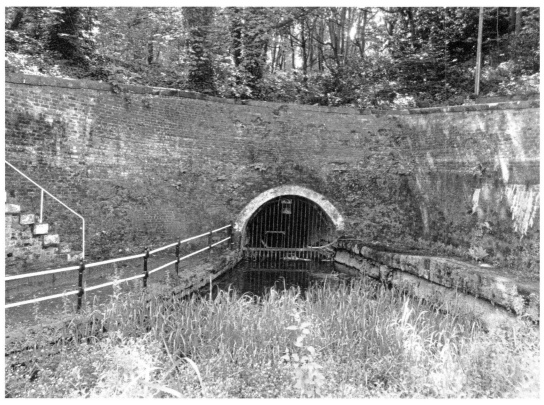

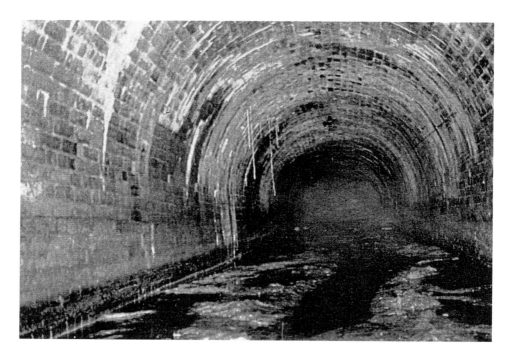

Inside Brindley's Tunnel

In 1979 two Olympic canoeists, Jon Goodwin and Robin Witter, decided to explore the now dangerous tunnel. They managed to get to the middle but found it blocked. They went then to the other end and explored from there. Fortunately they were able to take a remarkable series of photographs, two of which appear here. The first view looks back at the south entrance of the tunnel; this was described by Revd Shaw in 1777 as 'like the glimmering of a star: very beautiful'. Both views show that this part of the tunnel is lined with bricks.

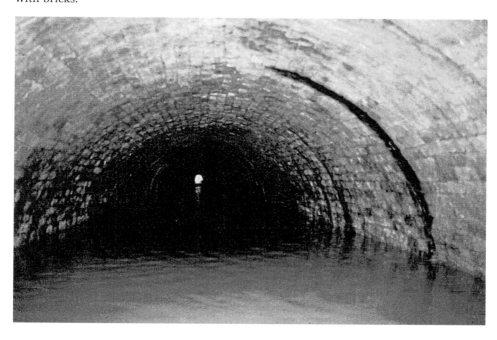

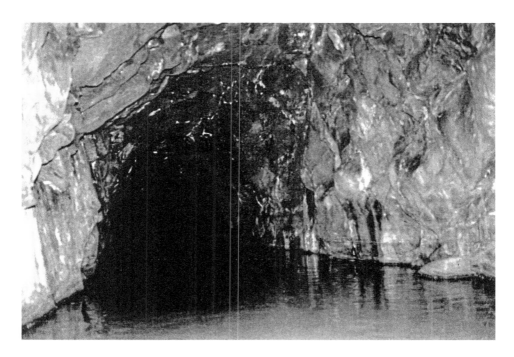

Inside Brindley's Tunnel

Brindley's Tunnel has natural rock as its lining. Stalactites have developed over the centuries. The pictures emphasise how low and how narrow the tunnel was for the barges and bargees. With no towpath, the boats were legged through – hard, poorly paid work. 'The men would lie on their backs, holding on by grasping boards underneath and their legs hanging over the water.' (Revd Llewellin). It took around two hours to leg a boat through, while the horses were taken over the hill via Boathorse Road.

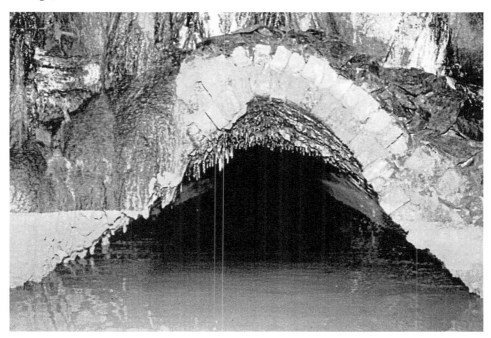

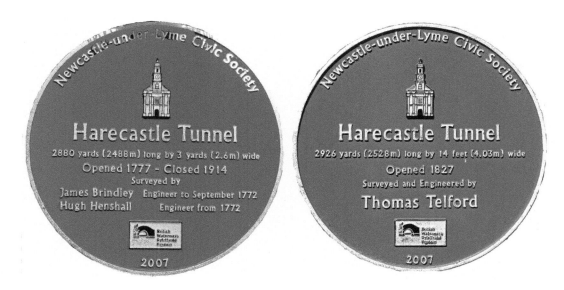

The Two Tunnels

Brindley's Tunnel was a tremendous engineering achievement. This was recognised at the time – it was described as 'the eighth wonder of the world' by a contemporary. It took eleven years to complete. It was a great success but soon proved unable to cope with the rapidly increasing traffic on the canal. The result was the building of a second tunnel, opened in 1827 and built by another great engineer, Thomas Telford. It was higher and wider, providing a towpath. The two plaques affixed to the canal keeper's office, show the details of the work of the two engineers. The recent picture shows Telford's tunnel to the left, Brindley's to the right.

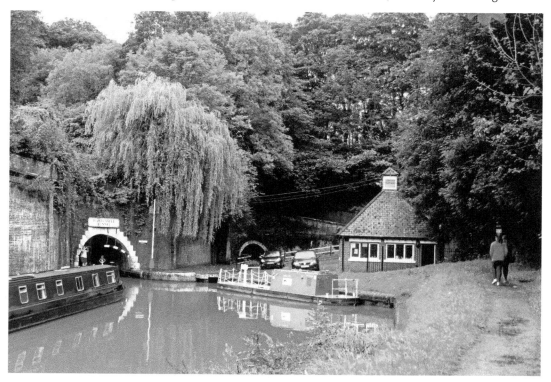

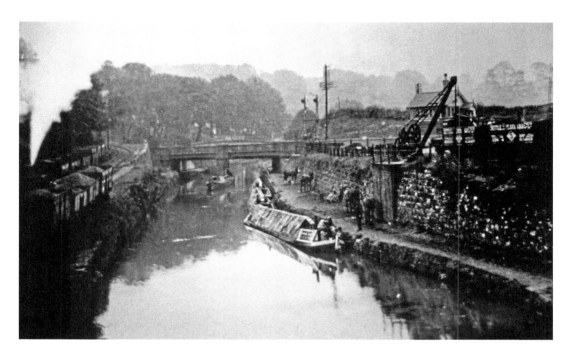

A Busy Canal

This photograph (from around 1910) captures the canal at a busy moment. The view is towards the two tunnels (Brindley's is still open) and the two bridges, with the railway bridge and the canal bridge behind it. Coal is being loaded onto a barge on the right, while full trucks pass by on the left. The horses that pull the barges are pictured, resting on the right. The canal is still busy today, especially in the summer, but carries holidaymakers rather than coal. The recent picture is taken from a similar viewpoint – towards the bridges and tunnel entrances.

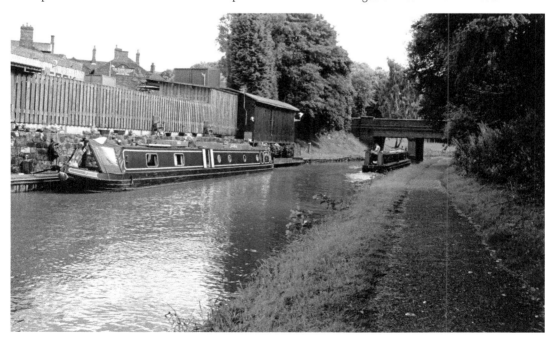

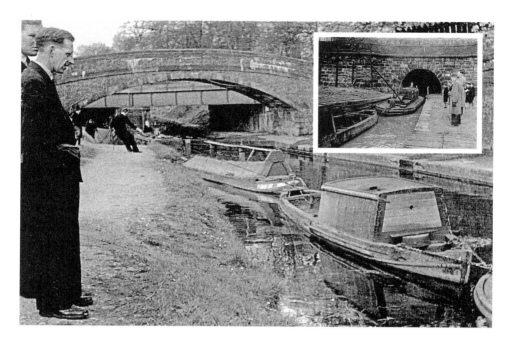

An Electric Tug

From around 1914 an interesting way of taking loaded barges through the Telford Tunnel was by using an electric tug. This photograph shows a line of boats, which would be attached to the electric tug and pulled through on a shift system. The photograph is taken from the entrance to the tunnel, towards the canal bridge with the railway bridge behind it. The system was being demonstrated to a group in the 1970s. The inset shows the electric tug at the Chatterley (southern) end of the Telford Tunnel. Now barges move under their own power and the electric tug has joined legging and the use of horses as historical curiosities on the canals.

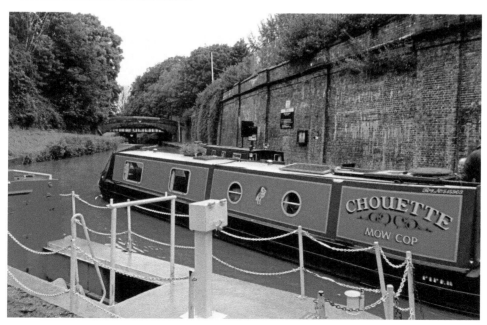

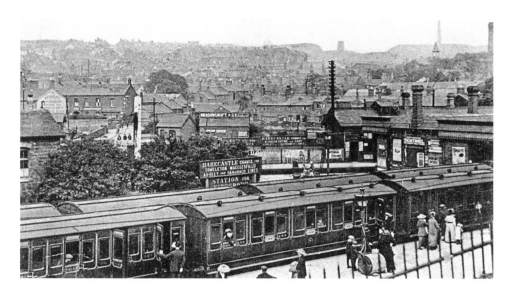

Kidsgrove Station

Kidsgrove Station was the most northernly station on the Staffordshire on the Potteries mainline of the North Staffordshire Railway (opened in 1848). Its name has changed several times; originally Harecastle Station, it was renamed Kidsgrove Central in 1944, with the 'Central' dropped in 1964. It was an important junction, with the main line, dividing on the right to Macclesfield and on the left to Crewe. The wonderfully detailed photograph (early 1900s) shows a busy station, with boards advertising the destinations on the two branches of the main line. The background shows chimneys of Birchenwood. Then there is a view of the town, with the clock tower of the town hall visible. The modern photograph shows the station at a quiet time of day with a train at the platform on the Crewe line.

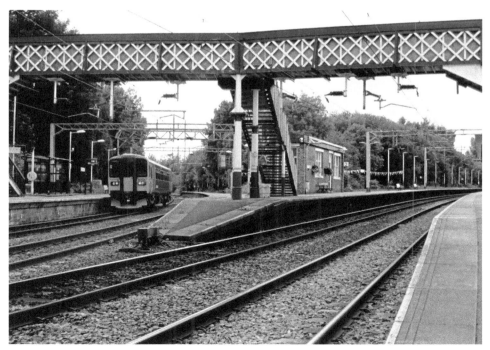

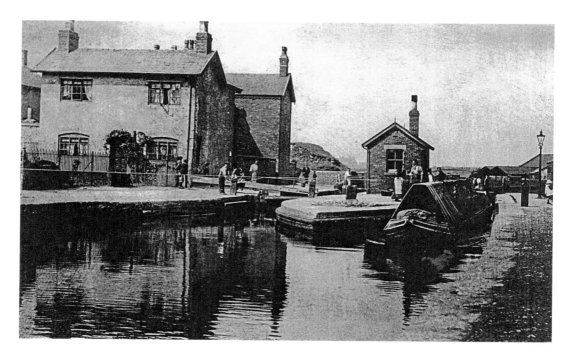

Plants Locks, Hardingswood

Hardingswood was an important area in Kidsgrove's growth as an industrial town. Dr Plot, in *A Natural History of Staffordshire* (1686), noted that coal was being mined here. Gilbert's house (Whitehall) overlooked Hardingswood, where he had a coal wharf. In 1831 the newly built Macclesfield Canal joined the Trent Mersey at Plants Locks. The busy scene in the early photograph shows the locks, with the lock-keeper's house on the left. The lock-keeper, Mr Groom, occupied it for over sixty years. The house has now gone but otherwise the scene here is little changed.

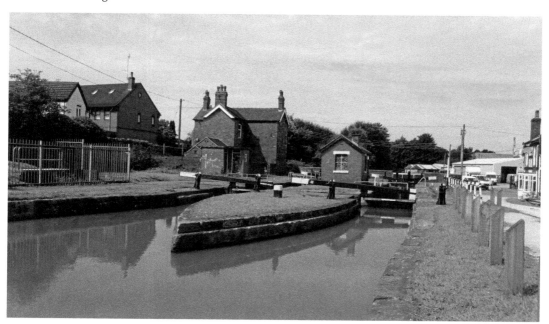

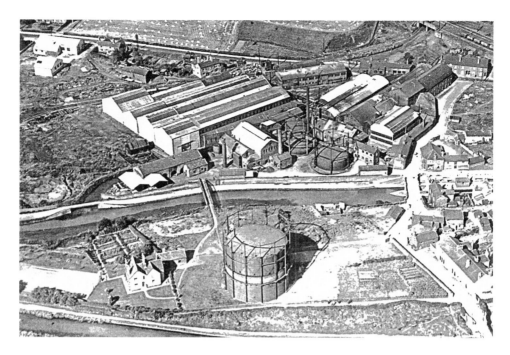

Industry by the Canal

Tourism has become the main industry of the canal but the area near Plant Locks is still a busy one, as the recent picture shows. The railway and then road transport took the movement of heavy goods from the canals. The aerial view (from around 1934) shows the main-line railway at the top of the picture and the A50 through Kidsgrove. The gasometers have become redundant, though the building that still bears the sign of the company remains, visible on the right of the new photograph. It reads 'The Kidsgrove Gaslight Company Founded 1888 Warehouse 189? John Gater Chairman.' The Trent Mersey Canal runs across the centre of the aerial picture while the Macclesfield Canal is in the foreground.

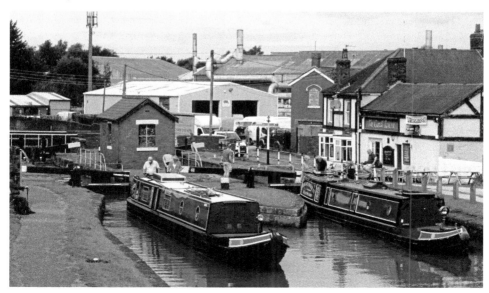

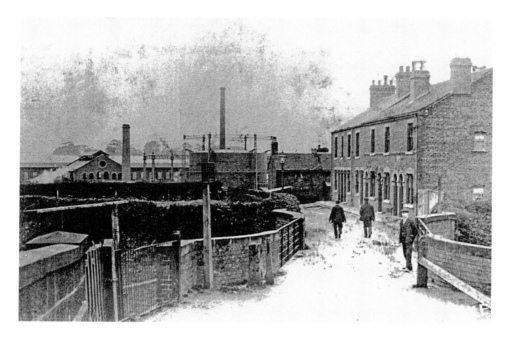

Hardingswood, Bridge over the Macclesfield Canal

The Macclesfield Canal (1831), another canal designed by Telford, joins with the Trent & Mersey Canal at Hardingswood. It runs under the bridge shown here and then parallel with it until it crosses it by an aqueduct. It then proceeds on its way towards the Cheshire towns of Congleton and Macclesfield. In the background is a gasometer and some of the industrial buildings facing Plants Locks around the corner. That view is entirely obliterated by the trees on the left in the new photograph. The terrace of houses on the right is still there.

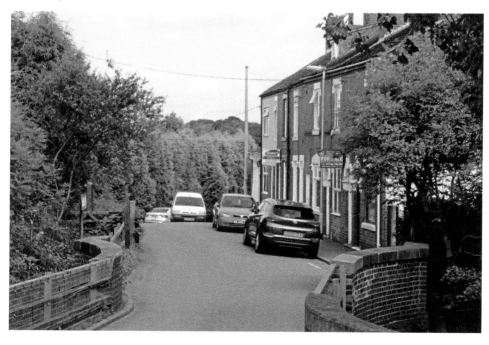

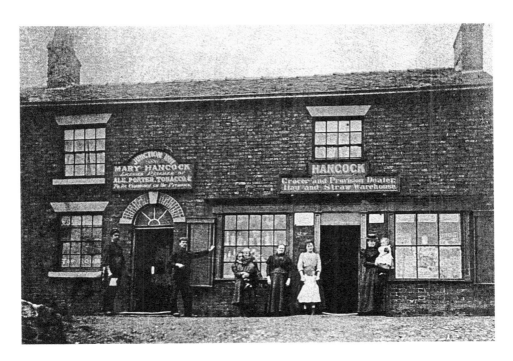

The Junction Inn

Canal work was obviously thirsty work – this is one of the three pubs alongside the canal at the Hardingswood locks. Mrs Hancock, the landlady, in the middle of the picture, also owned the stores. As well as groceries, the sign advertises a hay and straw warehouse – a reminder of the needs of the canal horses which could also be stabled a little further on to the left of the inn. These buildings remain today, converted into housing. The leggers frequented the inn which was apparently referred to as the 'swinging plank'.

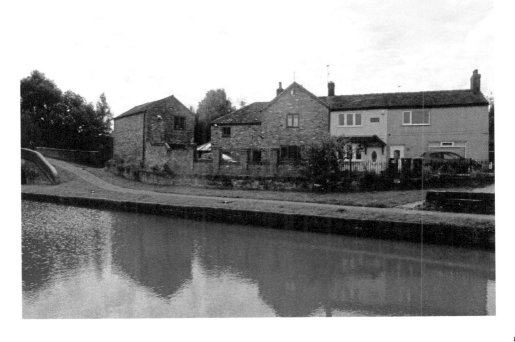

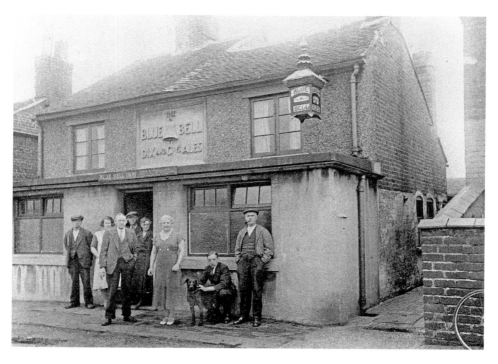

The Bluebell

Next to the Junction Inn and the stores is a second inn, the Bluebell, little changed in appearance and still open for business. A building to the left has gone and the former bowling green behind the pub is now a car park.

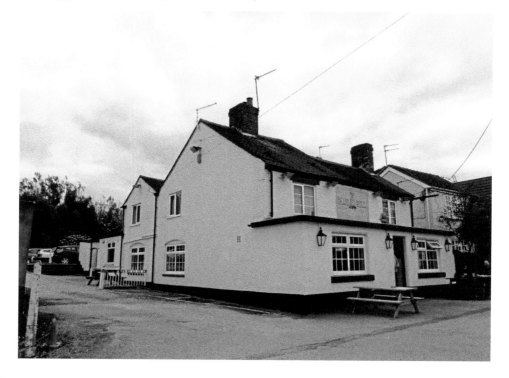

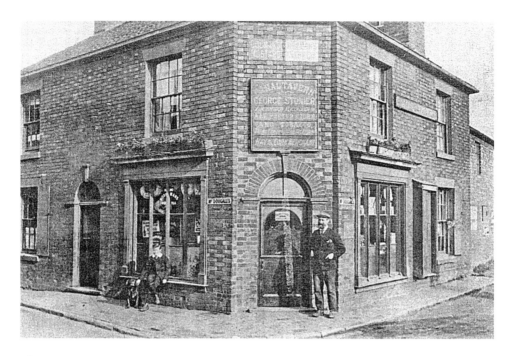

The Canal Tavern

The Canal Tavern on the other side of the locks is also still in business and clearly recognisable in the recent photograph. George Stonier, the landlord in 1904, stands outside below the sign that emphasises the need to cater for the canal horses. As well as the licensee, Mr Stonier is a hay and corn merchant. The Tavern now serves thirsty pleasure boaters rather than bargees.

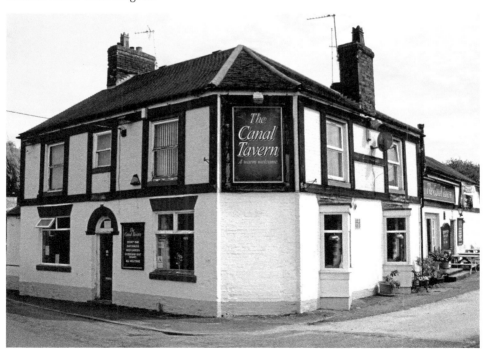

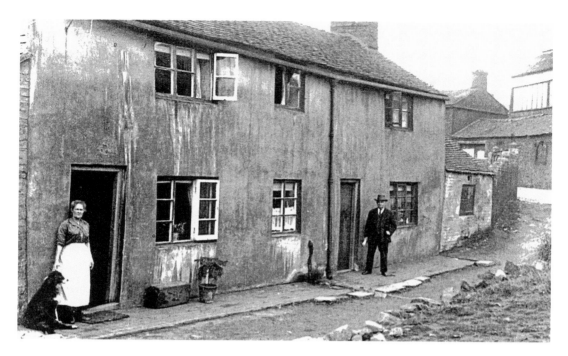

'Living Down the Hole' (1890s)

The poor housing conditions for some in Hardingswood in the late nineteenth century are shown in photograph above from around 1890. These houses were built beside the Canal Tavern, which is now its car park. The house on the left had two bedrooms, the house on the right had one. Canal 'leggers' often lived in what were described as 'cabins'. Kidsgrove's first Medical Officer of Health, the impressively named Dr Adolphus Great-Rex, reported in 1874 that forty people, who inhabited nine houses, shared 'only 2 privies'. He was still complaining in 1912 of 'damp, dilapidated housing'. (Philip Leese).

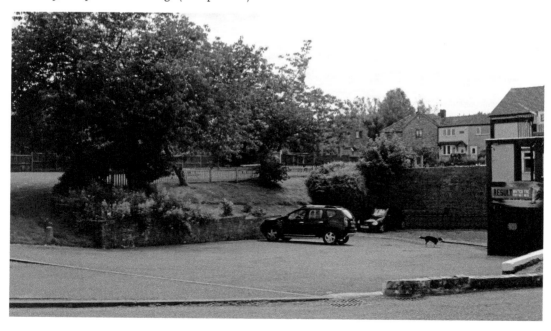

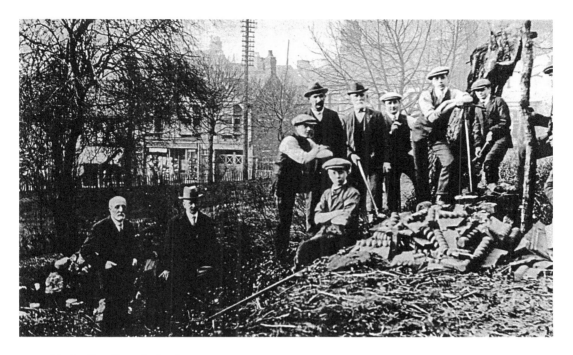

Methodist Chapel, the Avenue

The first building on the corner of Liverpool Road and the Avenue is the Wesleyan Methodist Chapel. The old photograph shows the beginning of the building of the new chapel – 'putting in the footings'. In the background is a part of the Co-op building in the centre of the town. The large and impressive buildings that were started in the 1920s, shown in the recent picture, are now unused and up for sale. In the few weeks since taking this photograph, a solicitors' office has moved into a part of the building.

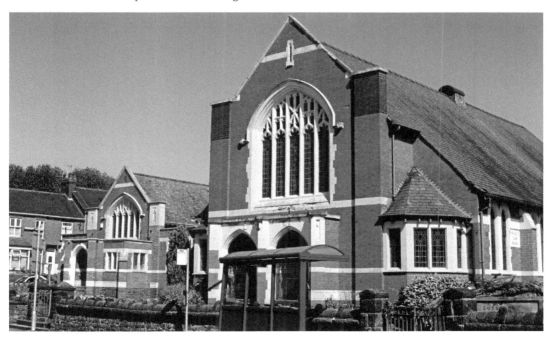

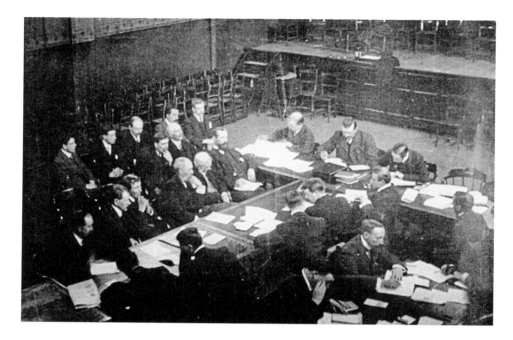

St Johns Wood Road

Just past the Catholic church and school is the turning into St Johns Wood Road. As the recent photograph shows, this road retains its late Victorian appearance. The date of 1893 appears still on the first house on the left. This quiet road was, however, the scene of a gruesome murder. In a substantial villa, later demolished, a mother, daughter and their maid were murdered. A rare photograph of the subsequent coroner's court (1911) in the Town Hall has survived. The murderer, whose motive appeared to be robbery, was tried and found guilty but also insane, and detained at His Majesty's pleasure.

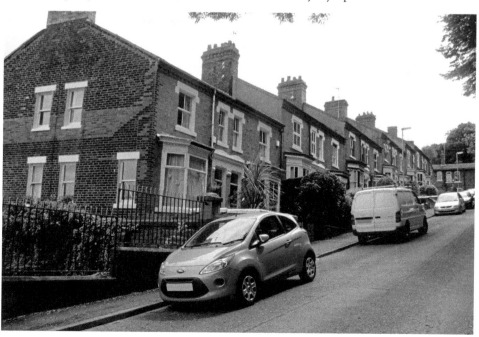

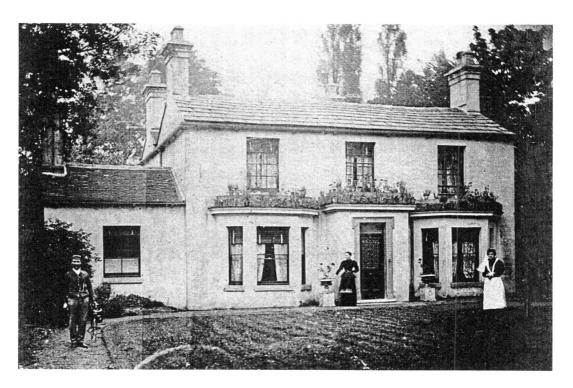

Ravenswood House

From this point the Avenue takes on the more peaceful appearance of the nineteenth century, described in 1875 as 'a lovely carriageway, situated in the lower part of the town ... the visitor is astonished at the rural beauty of the surrounding scenery.' The 'carriageway' was in fact a carriage drive leading to Clough Hall. Ravenswood was one of a number of substantial properties along this part of the avenue. It was a doctors' surgery in the early twentieth century and is now a residential home for the elderly.

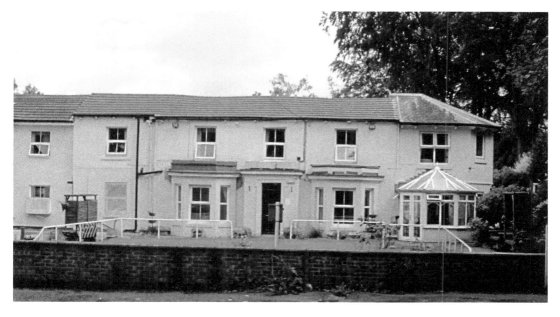

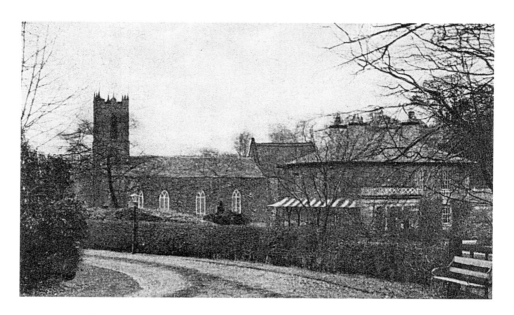

St Thomas Church, 1837

In fast growing industrial towns like Kidsgrove, the Church of England was anxious to build new churches to provide for the increasing population. The church was also aware of the increasing competition of Methodism, especially in mining areas. Like other wealthy landowners and industrialists in the nineteenth century, the Kinnersleys of Clough Hall were willing to provide the funds for a church, a vicarage and a school. The Kinnersleys went further in the case of St Thomas's; it appears that the church was built to Mrs Kinnersley's design. After Thomas Kinnersley's death in 1855, his wife had a chancel added to the church in his memory. Consecrated in 1858, it was designed by the renowned Victorian church architect Gilbert Scott.

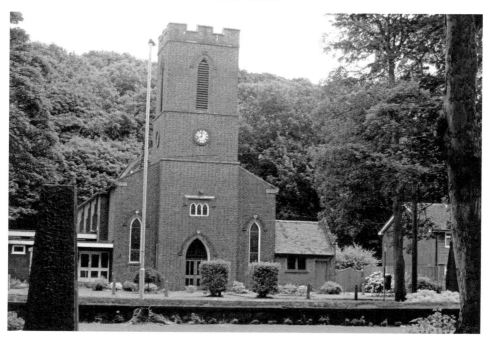

The Reverend Frederick Wade

Frederick Wade was the vicar of Kidsgrove from 1837 until 1880. He quickly established a reputation as an active priest with a strong personality. He saw the importance of education and, in 1839, a church school was built, funded by Thomas Kinnersley. This later became the Kinnersley Memorial School on Liverpool Road. Wade was anxious to improve moral standards and claimed success: 'the people are more regular in their devotional exercises, steady and domesticated at home, industrious and hardworking ... and respectful and obedient to their superiors.' However, he did not always succeed. A young man told a commissioner in 1842 'Mr Wade talks to us sometoimes and tells us to be good. I sometoimes take his advoice – sometoimes I dinna.' Wade is buried in the cemetery behind the site of the Memorial School; the inscription on his grave includes these words, 'at his own request his remains are laid among the people he loved so long.'

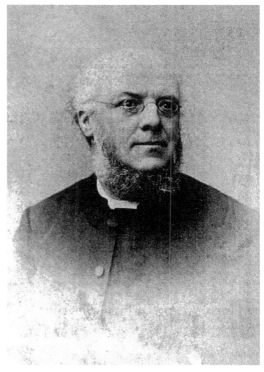

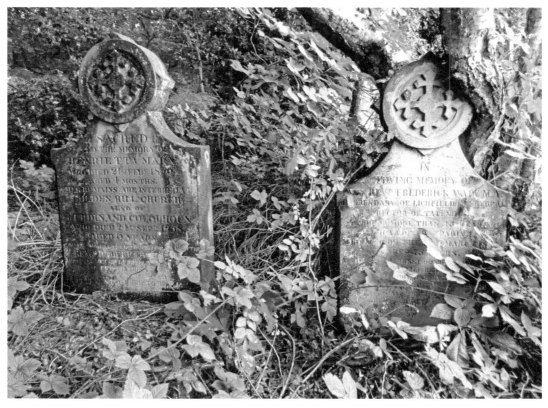

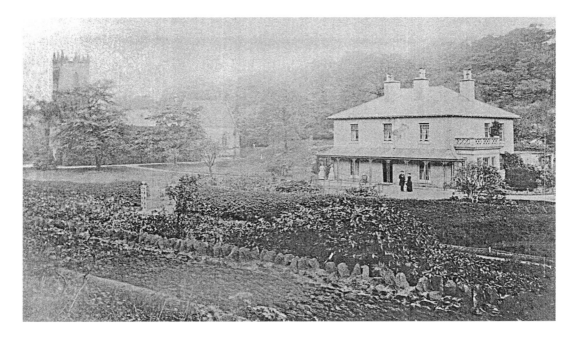

The Vicarage

The old vicarage was a large and attractive building. It was 'one of the prettiest clerical houses in Staffordshire ... with an old-world garden rich in rhododendrons, laburnums, azaleas as well as pear, plum and apple trees' (Revd Llewellin). He adds that 'in the old days, the gardeners came down from Clough Hall to attend the vicar's garden – good old days were those!' He also comments on the servants who are shown in the picture with the vicar, Revd Hicks. He kept four servants 'to the amazement of this neighbourhood'. All has changed now: the old vicarage has been replaced by a modern house, while the garden has disappeared under other housing.

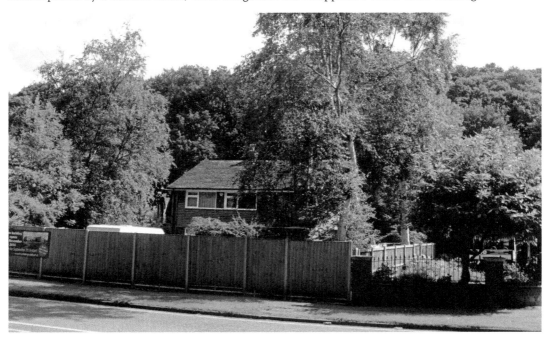

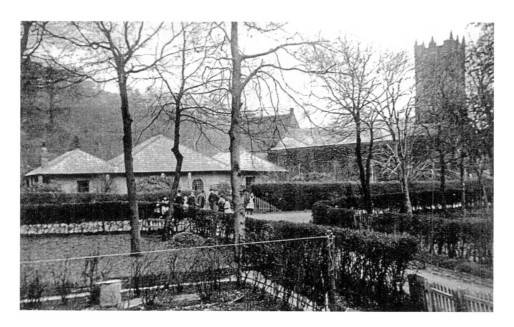

The Wade Centre

The present site of the Wade Centre started life as a church school. In 1875 it was described as 'one of the prettiest little slapdashed schools that could possibly be imagined; buried as it were in flowers, ferns and greenery.' According to Revd Llewellin in 1909, 'the Avenue Church School, erected in 1837, at the expense of Squire Kinnersley, was taken down and an improved school built on the site. It was not much larger but it is better equipped in every way.' It was later used as a girls' school and as an infant's school. This is the building we now see in the recent photograph. The present Wade Centre is used as a nursery school and community centre.

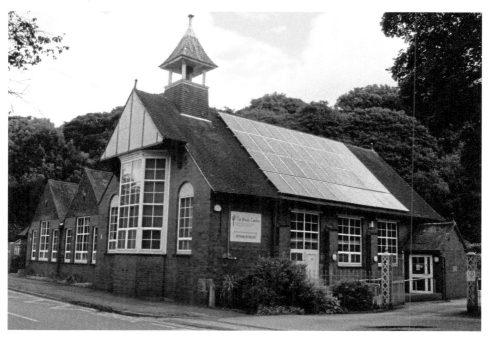

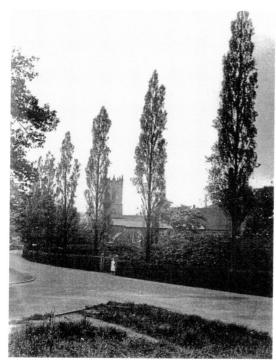

The Twelve Apostles
The twelve poplar trees shown in the picture to the right, probably taken between the wars, were an attractive feature of the Avenue. They were known as 'the twelve apostles'. While the poplars have gone, this part of the Avenue retains an attractive tree-lined aspect.

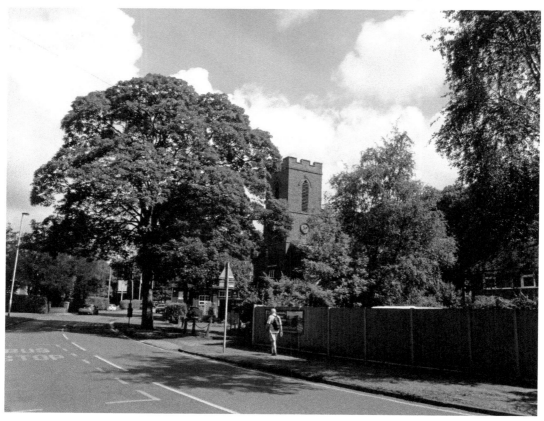

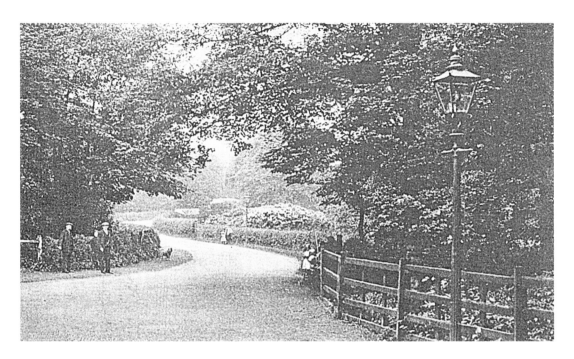

A View Along the Avenue

These photographs were taken from the junction of the Avenue and Boathorse Road. They reveal a view that is both attractive and, in spite of the long span of time they cover, not very different. As the name suggests, Boathorse Road was the route taken by bargees with their horses to the Chatterley end of the Harecastle Tunnel. As they crossed over the hill, the barges were being 'legged' through the tunnel.

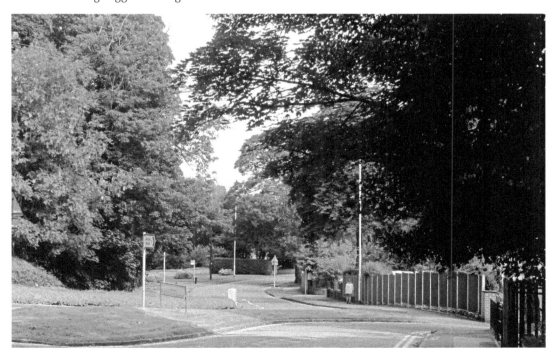

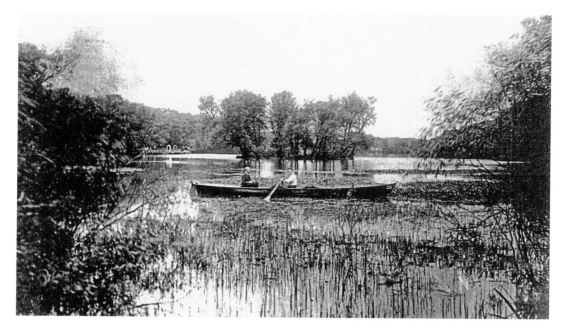

Bathpool

Boathorse Road leads to Bathpool, a popular recreation area. It was acquired by Kidsgrove Council after the closure of the Clough Hall Park and Gardens in 1904. The idyllic scene in the old photograph shows the pool at about this time. As the recent picture indicates, the pool is still an attractive feature. However, the whole area saw a tremendous upheaval in the 1960s, brought about by the rerouting of the main-line railway through Bathpool. The pool was 'reshaped' and given a sharper, concreted edge. Peace and quiet is regularly disturbed by trains rushing through the cutting close by and just visible in the recent photograph.

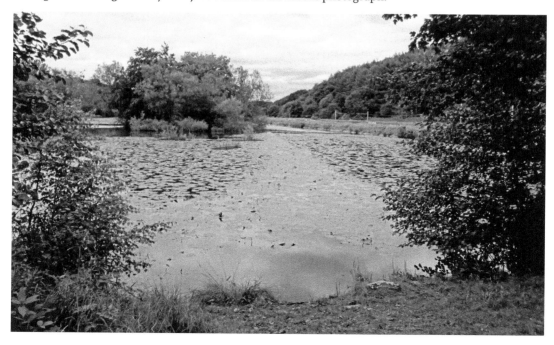

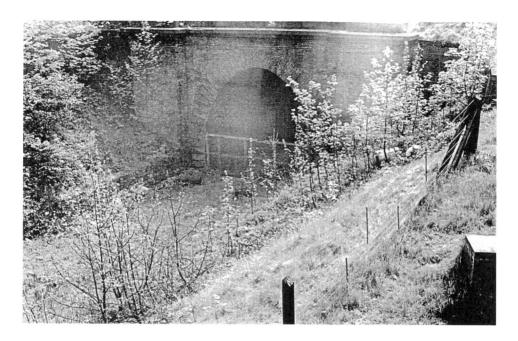

Bathpool and the Railway

The recent photograph shows the main line from Kidsgrove to Stoke, now diverted from its old route and running through Bathpool. The electrification of the line exposed weaknesses in the old route, which went through three tunnels. These were found to be in bad condition and so a diversion of over 2 miles was built, including the tunnel and cutting shown here. The work was carried out against stiff local opposition and opened in 1966. A photograph from the 1970s shows the mouth of the disused middle tunnel on the old route.

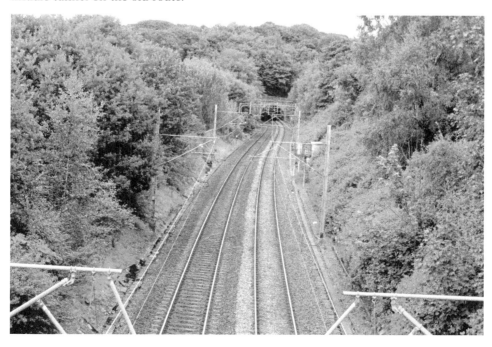

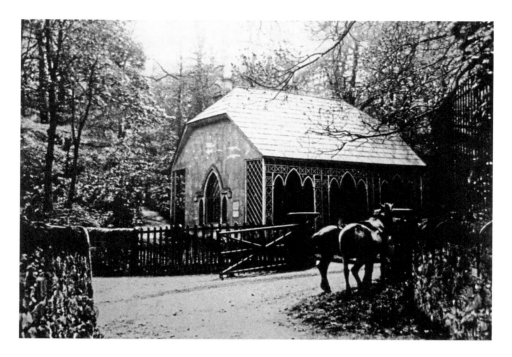

Clough Hall, the Lodge on the Avenue

The modern house, behind the lush vegetation, is one of the surviving lodges of the Clough Hall estate. Only a small part of the present building is visible, as a reminder of the old lodge. Approached along the Avenue, the lodge had gates through which guests, arriving in their horse-drawn carriages, could be admitted. Later photographs of the lodge show it in a very dilapidated state before modernisation took place.

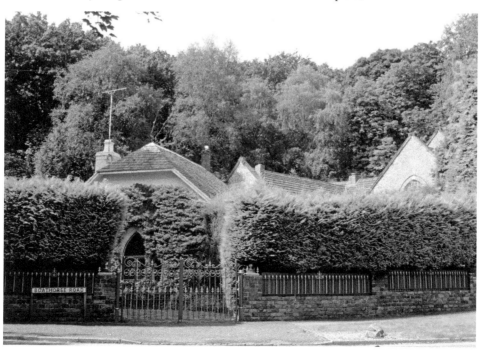

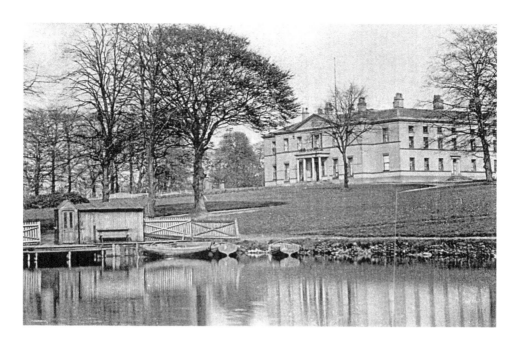

Clough Hall

It was the Gilbert family who first purchased the Clough Hall estate and built the impressive building shown in the old photograph. An older Clough Hall, built in the seventeenth century, was demolished and the new one replaced it just before the end of the eighteenth century. It was described as having 'twenty bedrooms and the luxury of mahogany in all the downstairs rooms'. The building was set in extensive parkland with a walled kitchen garden and an ornamental lake. After Gilbert's death in 1811, Clough Hall and its lands were purchased by the Kinnersley family, wealthy Newcastle bankers and hat manufacturers. It was Thomas Kinnersley who dominated the life of Kidsgrove until his death in 1855. The house was demolished in the 1920s and new housing now covers the site.

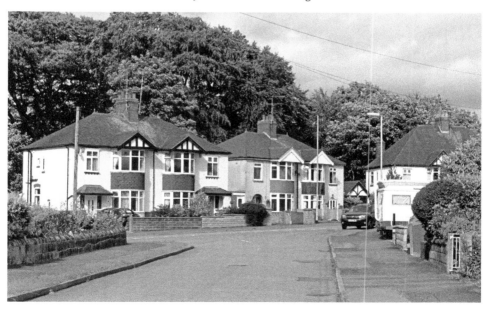

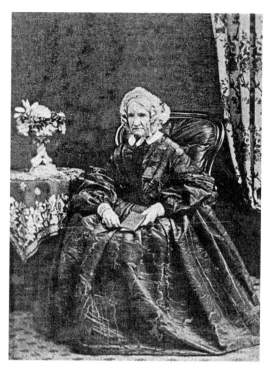

Esther Burgess, the Housekeeper

There are no portraits of either Thomas or Mrs Kinnersley in spite of their importance to the history of Kidsgrove. There is one portrait of a Clough Hall resident, Esther Burgess, who was the housekeeper there. Apart from that fact, the only information about her seems to be the inscription on her gravestone:

In affectionate memory of Esther Burgess
of Clough Hall who died 18 March 1878
aged 71 years
She was for many years the faithful
servant and friend of the late
Mrs Kinnersley
Well done thou good and faithful
servant
Enter thou into the joy of the Lord

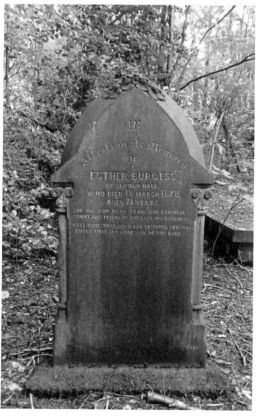

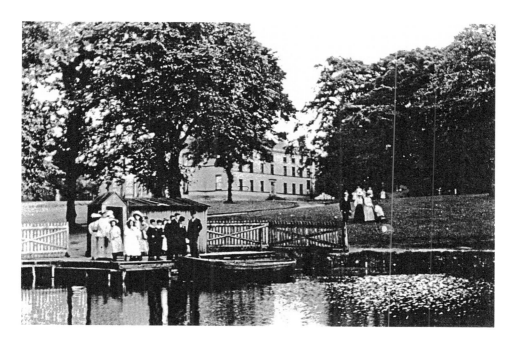

Clough Hall Lake

The extensive grounds of the Clough Hall estate included a large ornamental lake. A small section of the lake has survived between a row of houses and a row of bungalows. Clough Hall and its grounds deteriorated after the deaths of Mrs Kinnersley in 1877 and her niece, who inherited the property in 1879. The Kinnersleys' business interests were sold in the same period. Later a group of Manchester businessmen bought the estate with grandiose plans to turn it into pleasure gardens. The lake became a major feature of the scheme.

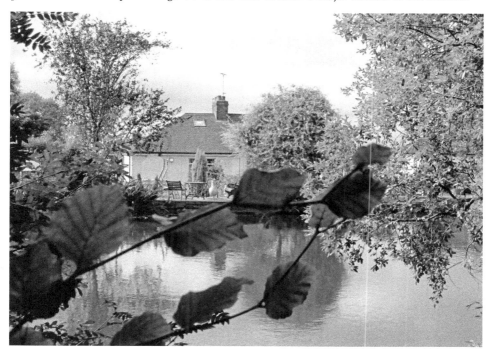

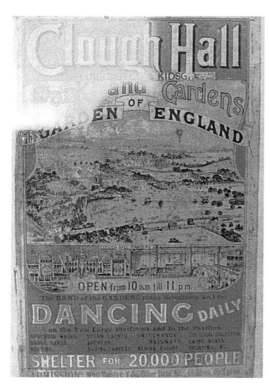

'The Paradise of the Potteries'

Advertised as 'The Paradise of the Potteries', the gardens were given a grand opening in 1890, featuring among many acts the famous French tightrope walker, Blondin. Some idea of the regular attractions put before a curious public are contained in this poster (possibly from 1900) which has, amazingly, survived. Open from 10 a.m. to 11 p.m. there is a band and 'Dancing Daily', splendid walks, large lakes with boating, switchback railways, aerial flight – the list goes on! There is also shelter for 2,000 people. Admission was '1 shilling on Whit Monday, other days 6d, children half price'. The recent picture is of a much reduced Clough Hall Park.

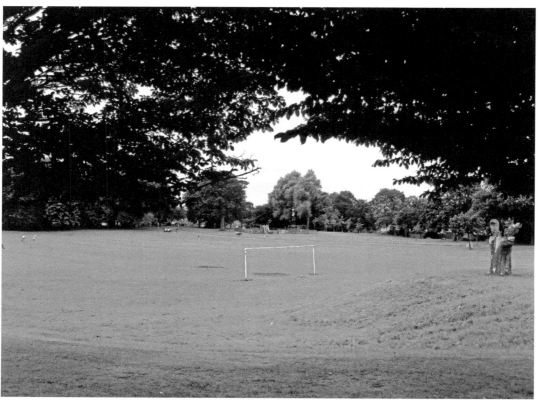

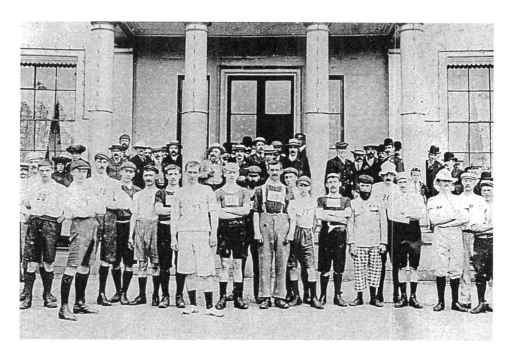

An Event at the Pleasure Grounds

Various sporting and other public events took place in the gardens. Here competitors are assembling outside Clough Hall for a 'walking match'. Not a serious event, it shows that the comic dress of many modern marathon runners has antecedents as early as 1900. The modern Clough Hall Park provides some more limited space for sports, a children's playground and other outdoor activities. In spite of all its advertised attractions, the 'Paradise of the Potteries' was short lived. Numbers declined and the gardens closed by 1905. The hall lingered on until its demolition in the 1920s.

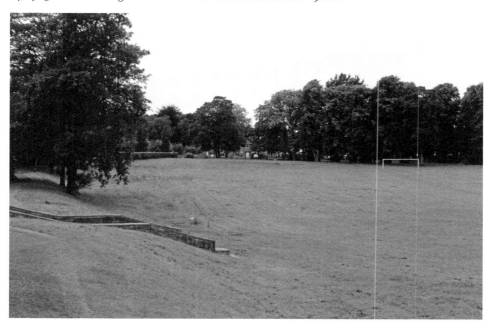

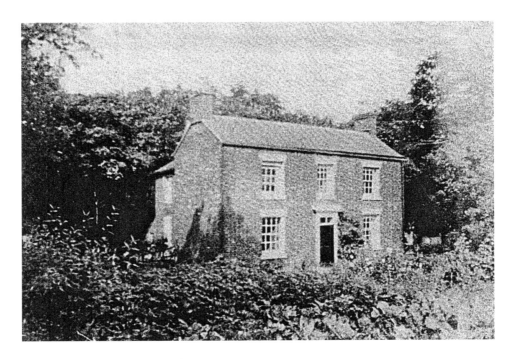

The Garden Cottage, Kinnersley Avenue

Another survivor of the Clough Hall estate is the Garden Cottage. It was occupied for over forty years by James Henderson during the nineteenth century. He was the head gardener of the estate: 'he was master of the nearby walled vegetable garden with its hothouses, flower beds, rose garden and shrubberies. At the age of 74 he was still in charge, assisted by his 50 year-old son'. The two pictures show the house as Henderson would have known it and the present house, clearly modernised but readily recognisable.

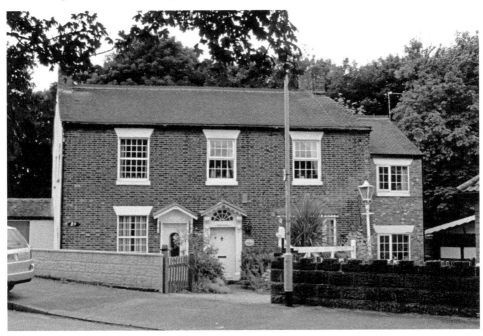

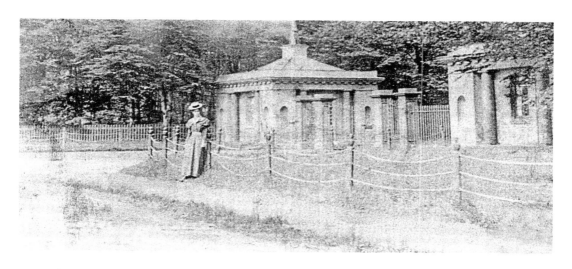

Clough Hall Lodges

These two lodges are situated on the busy A34 road and were probably built in the 1820s. They are very well preserved, especially the southern lodge on the right. This building, Grade II listed, has been very well restored by the Staffordshire Buildings Trust. The old photograph (from around 1900) shows what is missing in the modern picture: the pillars, wrought-iron gates, railings and chain fence. The gates would be opened by the wives of the families that lived here. The husbands would usually work in the Kinnersley mines or ironworks. The only puzzle is how a family fitted into such small buildings, originally with only two rooms.

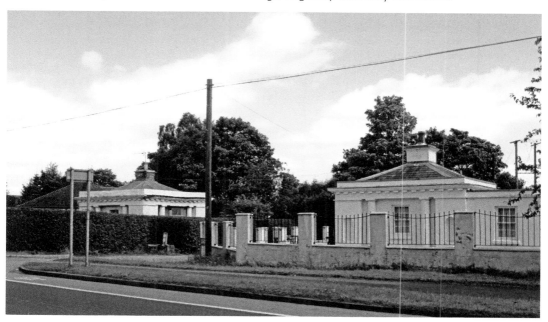

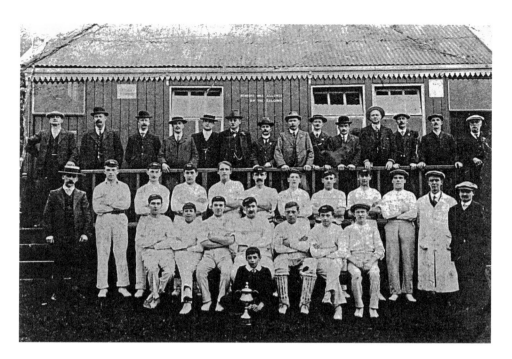

Kidsgrove Cricket Club

Kidsgrove Cricket Club was established in 1874 as Clough Hall Cricket Club and was granted use of Windmill Field by Mrs Kinnersley. In 1890 the club moved to its present ground, part of the new Pleasure Gardens by then. In 1913 the club changed its name to the present Kidsgrove Cricket Club. The team photograph was taken in the 1930s, in front of the pavilion. Only members of the club were allowed stand on the balcony, as the notice makes clear. The present facilities of the club are on a rather grander scale as the recent photograph shows.

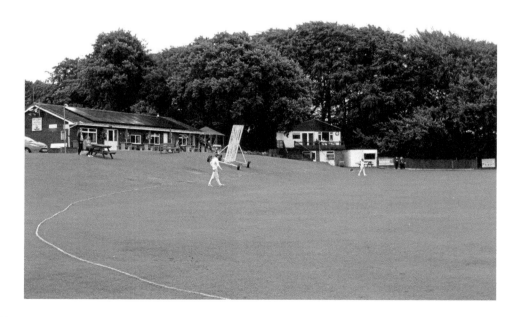

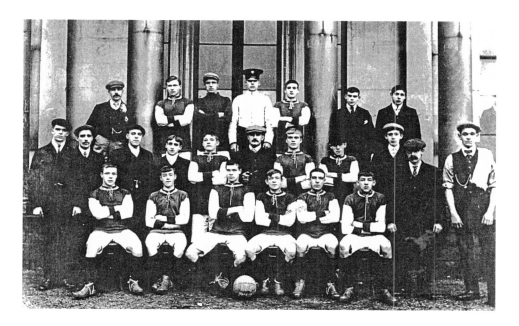

Kidsgrove Athletic FC

Kidsgrove Athletic FC appears to have two lives. The present club was formed in 1952 at a meeting in the Bluebell public house in Hardingswood. A raffle was held and it raised 13s (65p)! Since those unpromising beginnings, the club has moved up through a number of leagues to its present status in the Evo Stick League, Northern Premier, First Division South. The club plays at the modern Novus Stadium, shown in the photograph. However, there was an earlier club of the same name. The team photograph (from around 1909) shows that team with their president, trainer and other officials. They appear to have played in the grounds of the old Clough Hall estate. They have been photographed outside the front of the hall, now looking distinctly shabby and marked by graffiti. A shadowy figure in the window suggests the hall is still in use.

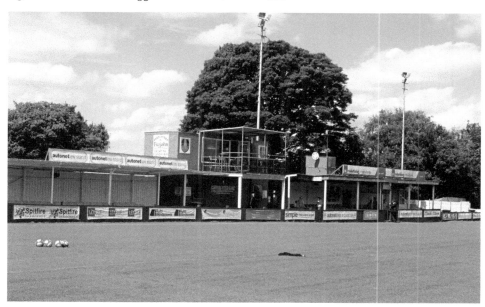

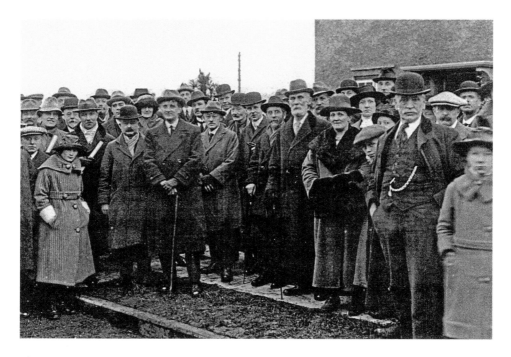

The Avenues

During the First World War, Lloyd George made his famous pledge to provide 'Homes fit for Heroes'. Housing Acts in 1919 and 1923 provided some government subsidies for house building, which Kidsgrove Urban District Council used to build the houses of the First, Second, Third and Fifth Avenues. These houses have survived the years well. The old photograph shows the opening ceremony of the first council house by the chairman of the council, W. H. Heath (with the walking stick on the left).

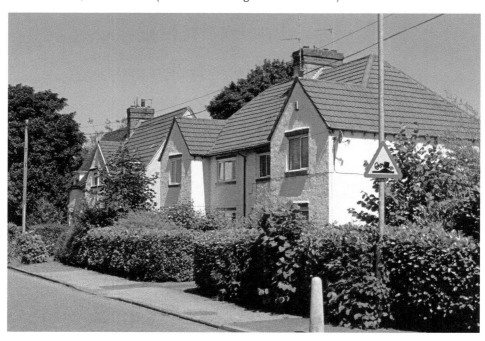

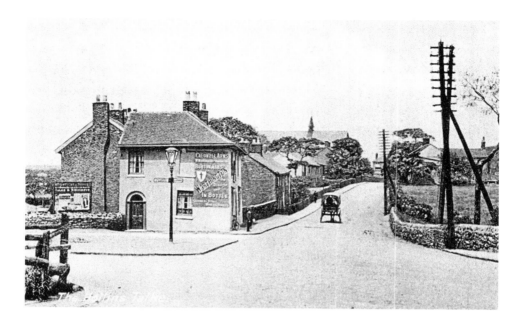

The Toby Inn, Formerly the Caldwell Arms

Named after the Caldwell family of nearby Linley Hall, this inn has been altered in both name and appearance since the nineteenth century. It stands at the Talke crossroads where the historic route to the North, the A34, turns right to go through Butt Lane. In 1714 it was the first road to be turnpiked in Staffordshire. The old photograph shows the inn in the 1920s. It took on its mock-Tudor design in the 1930s and new colouring in the 1940s. It is now a Toby Inn.

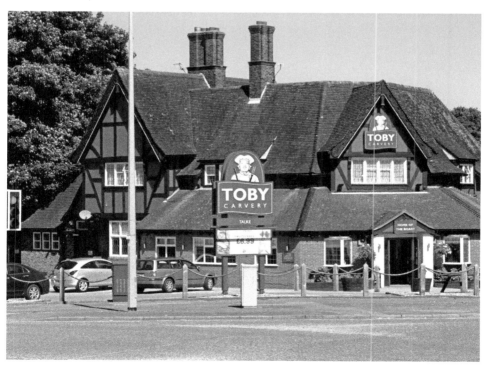

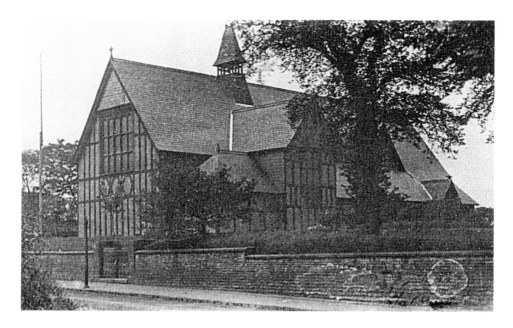

St Saviours Church

St Saviours was built 1878–89 to accommodate growing numbers from the expanding population of Butt Lane, then part of the parish of Talke. The parish church in Talke, St Martins, was too small so a new church was built, designed by London architect F. W. Hunt. It survived until 1971 when, with church attendances dwindling, it was demolished. 'This is a great pity; for the church was inventive and, though quite large, was decidedly human in scale and detail ... the three very large gabled dormers in the roof to allow light to stream in were a very happy idea'(N.Pevsner).

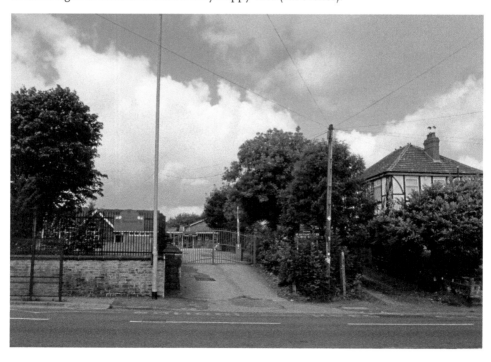

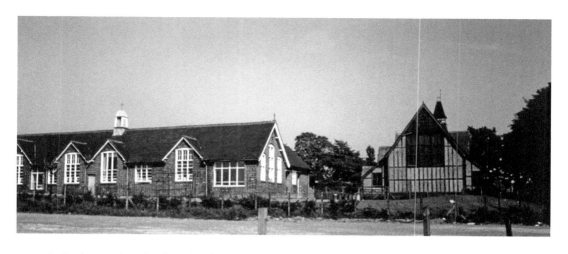

St Saviours Church of England Primary School

St Saviours Church of England Primary School replaced an older church (national) school situated in Old Butt Lane. The growth of population in the area had put additional pressure on the old Butt Lane school and its antiquated buildings. The new school was built in 1895, on land behind the church where it remains today. A small cross at the top of a gable is a reminder of the church that stood in front of the school. While the school retains much of its original appearance with the four gables on the side facing Congleton Road, the buildings have been extended to provide extra facilities.

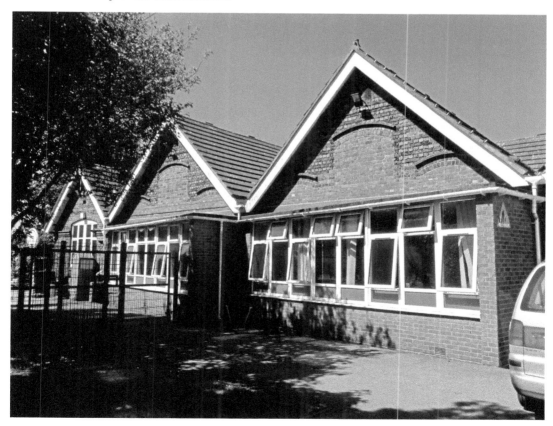

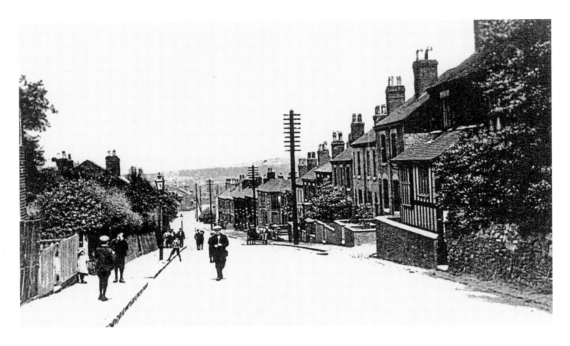

Congleton Road

Congleton Road is part of the A34 and, as the modern photograph shows, it is an extremely busy road through the centre of Butt Lane. The old photograph of the early twentieth century presents a much quieter picture, with people walking safely in the road and a horse-drawn vehicle. There is considerable continuity in the buildings on the right-hand side of the road, something that is true for much of Congleton Road. In spite of additions and external alterations to suit modern tastes, many of the houses keep much of their earlier appearance.

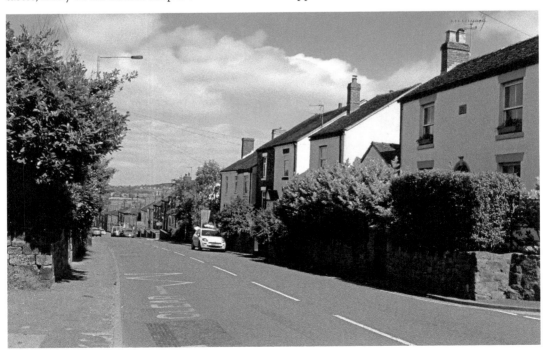

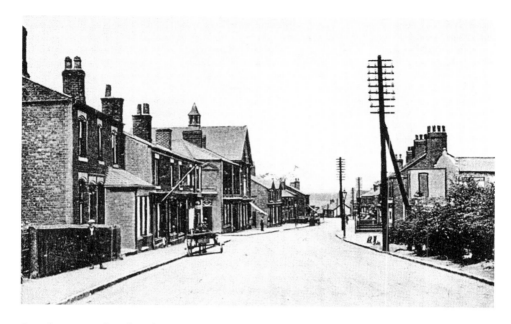

Congleton Road and Cedar Avenue

The view from further down Congleton Road in the recent picture shows an important change when compared to the photograph from around 1920. There is now a junction at which a right-hand turn, Cedar Avenue, takes travellers directly into Kidsgrove. This new route had long been mooted before action was taken in the 1920s. The new road was built and opened officially in 1928. Previously, Kidsgrove was reached by the longer route via Red Bull crossroads.

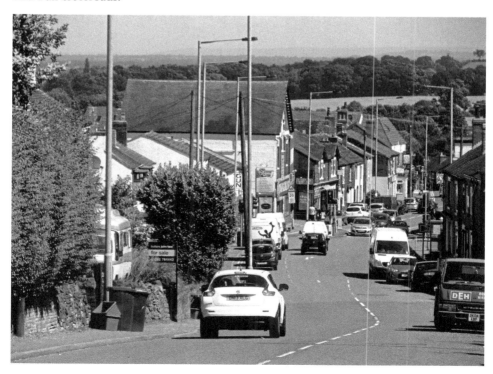

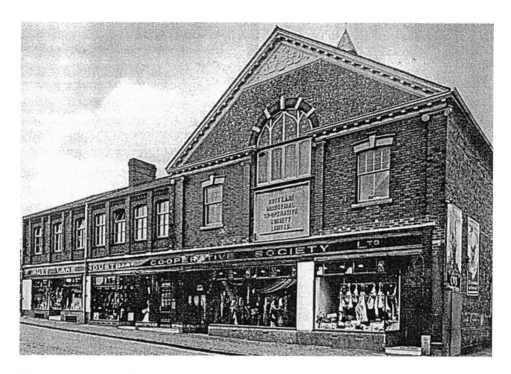

Butt Lane Co-operative Store

The first Butt Lane Co-op was opened in 1879. Its success soon meant larger premises were required and in 1891 a larger store was built at the junction of Congleton Road and Church Street. That building survives along with the plaque on its front. The building no longer houses the Co-op, as the modern photograph reveals. Behind the shop was a bakery, some walls of which remain. Butt Lane Co-operative Society flourished for many years and also played a part in social and political activities.

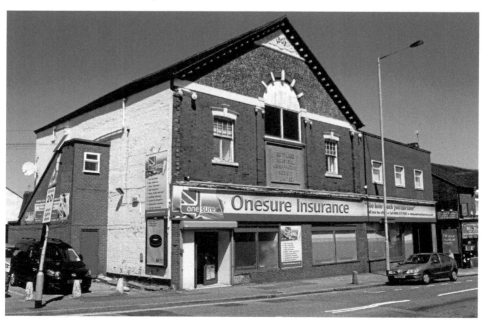

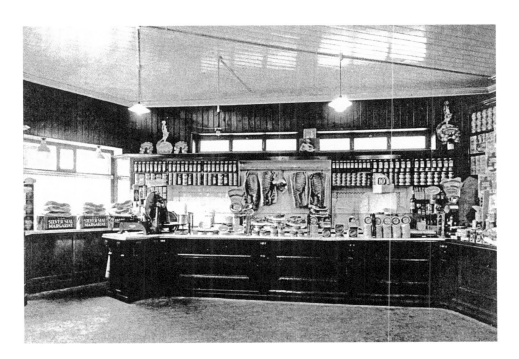

Butt Lane Co-operative Store

Some of the grandeur of the original Co-operative Store can be seen in the photograph of the interior of the grocery department (taken around 1930). However, like many other shops, the Co-op faced a new situation in the 1970s as new styles of shopping emerged. Large, out of town stores suited an increasingly car borne population. Co-operative societies merged and built supermarkets like the Co-operative Normid store at nearby Talke. More recently, individual local stores have come back in favour. The store in the new photograph shows the present shop, almost opposite the old one.

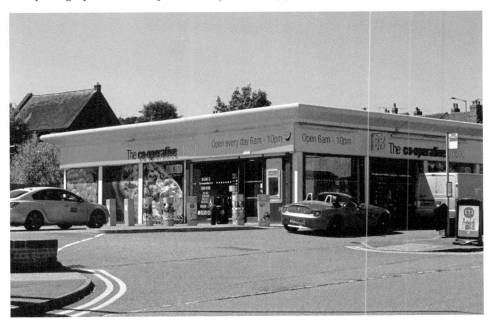

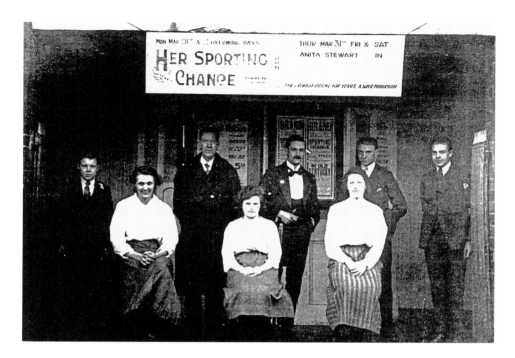

Cinema

Many small towns and even villages had their own cinema, long before the age of out-of-town complexes. Opened in 1911 as the Grand Picture House, it became the Regent in 1933 and flourished through 1940s and 1950s. The photograph from 1935 shows the eight members of staff at the cinema. As was usual at that time, the week's programme consisted of two films: Monday to Wednesday, you could see *Her Sporting Chance* ('Thrilling Drama'), then on Thursday to Saturday, *In Old Kentucky* ('the greatest picture for years- a super production'). The cinema closed in 1960 and became a bingo hall, a community centre called The Mustard Seed, a clothing factory and an Indian restaurant. It is now unused.

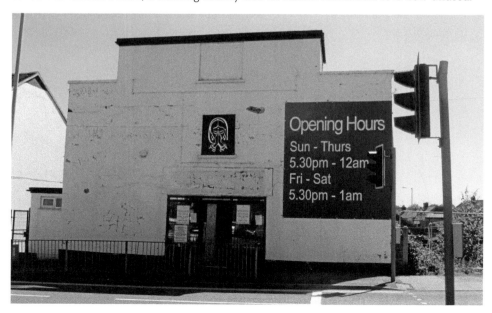

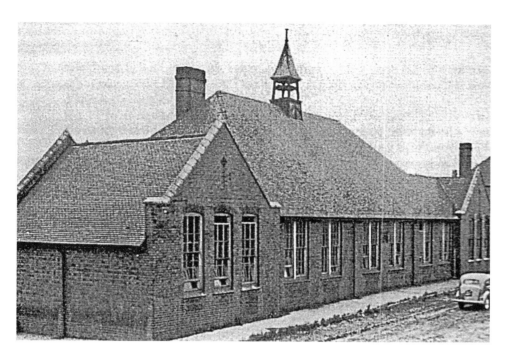

Reginald Mitchell CP School

Education passed into the hands of county councils in 1902 and, under these new powers, a new school was built on the Congleton Road – Butt Lane Council School, which opened in 1909. In the 1950s it was renamed the Reginald Mitchell CP School after the great aircraft designer. Before the building of the council school, children had been educated in a cramped area of the chapel in Chapel Street. The 1909 building is shown in the old photograph above. A former pupil of the old, cramped chapel school wrote 'we rejoiced in the well lit and airy classrooms, adequate cloakrooms and a corridor large enough to be used as a hall.'

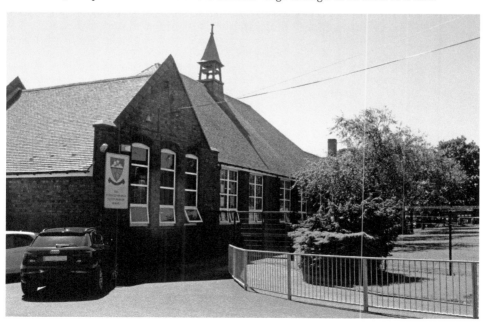

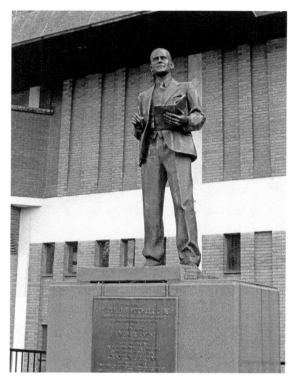

Reginald Mitchell's House

Reginald Mitchell, famous for designing the Spitfire, was born at No. 115 Congleton Road in 1895. His father was a headmaster at several schools, including the national school in Old Butt Lane. The family moved to Normacot in Stoke-on-Trent and Mitchell attended Hanley High School. His career in aircraft engineering took him to the Supermarine Aviation works in Southampton, where he proved to be an exceptional designer. The Spitfire, designed between in the mid-1930s, was described as a 'masterpiece of engineering'. He died in 1937, before the war in which his plane was to play such an important role.

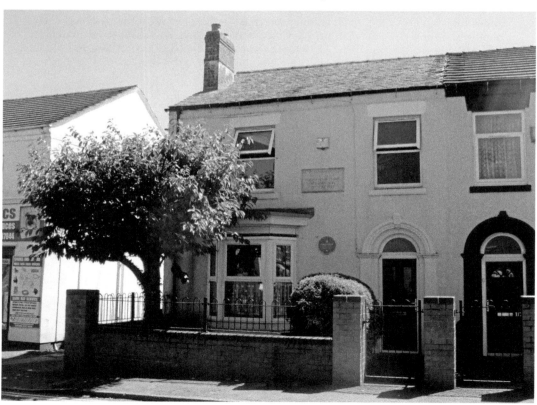

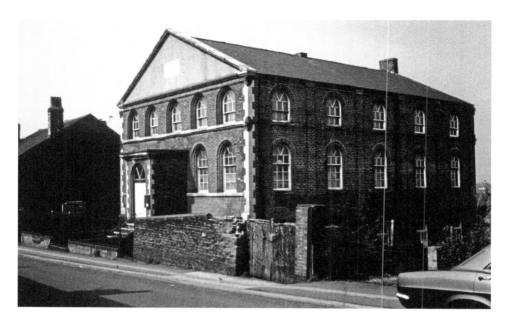

The Primitive Methodist Chapel (1869)

Primitive Methodism was strongest in mining areas like Butt Lane, and especially in an area so close to its origins at Mow Cop. This impressive three-storey building was not just a chapel but also housed a Sunday and a day school on its ground floor. It must have been a very cramped environment. A former pupil recalled that there was a galleried infant area, larger rooms for seniors, a hall holding three classes and two adjacent classrooms. The photograph shows the chapel in 1979. It was later demolished. Two chapels remain in Butt Lane: the Ebenezer Chapel (1873) on Banbury Street and the one pictured here, the Baptist Chapel on Church Street. This opened in 1886 and still thrives today.

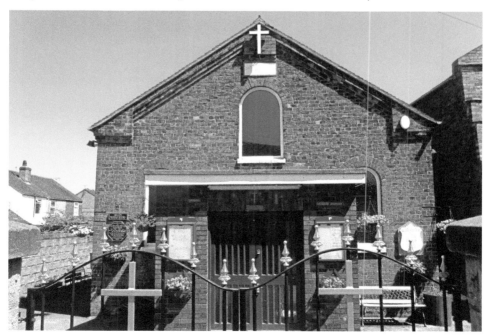

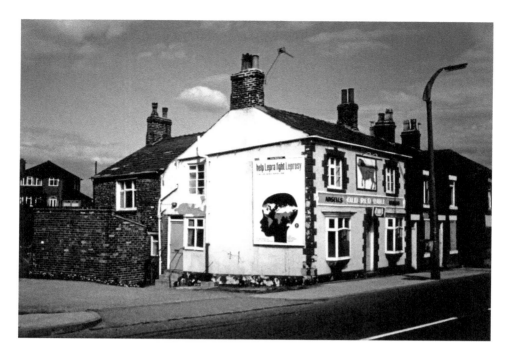

The Old Red Bull

The public house shown in the old photograph is one of two Red Bull public houses very near one another along Congleton Road. They were differentiated by locals as 'th'top bull' and 'th'bottom bull'. This building was probably the older of the two pubs. It closed in the 1970s. Since then it has served as a restaurant called Mrs B's Victorian Supper Rooms and is currently Masooms Massala, offering Indian and Bangladeshi cuisine.

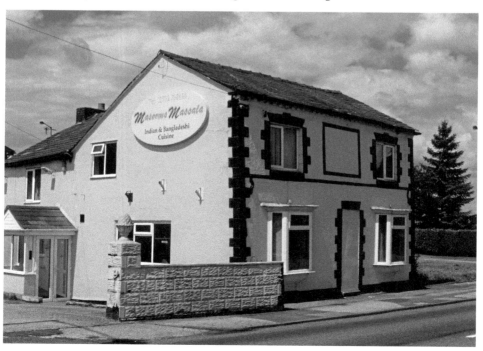

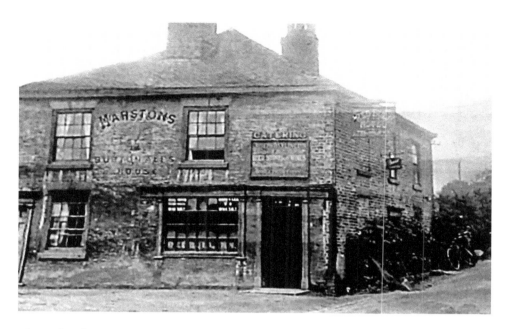

The Red Bull – 'Th'bottom Bull'

Situated just over the Cheshire county border, this Red Bull ('th'bottom bull') is in the advantageous position of being on two major communication routes, the Trent Mersey Canal and the busy A34. A warehouse was built by the transport firm Pickfords, at the wharf on the other side of the canal, and a small community grew up in the area. The inn was probably also used by miners and canal workers both to pick up their wages and quench their thirst. The old photograph, dated 1903, reveals a considerable change in the appearance of the inn.

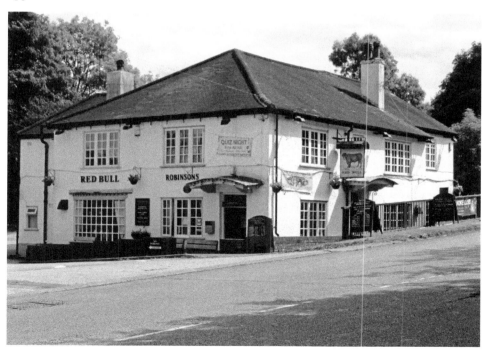

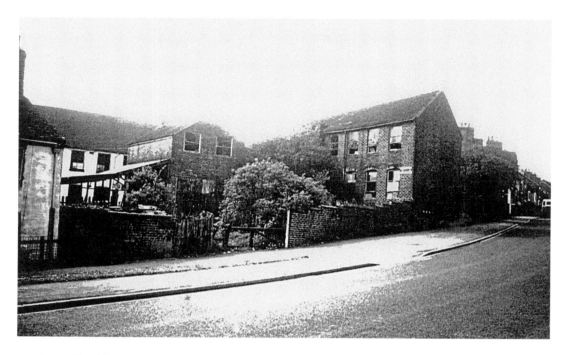

Fustian Mill, Old Butt Lane

The buildings in the old photograph, from 1979, show a fustian mill set up by Samuel Cope in the 1890s. Fustian is a velvet-like fabric made by cutting threads from long rolls of cotton. The mill employed about around forty women and continued working until the 1930s. The recent picture shows the only remaining building of the mill, which now houses a modern energy firm.

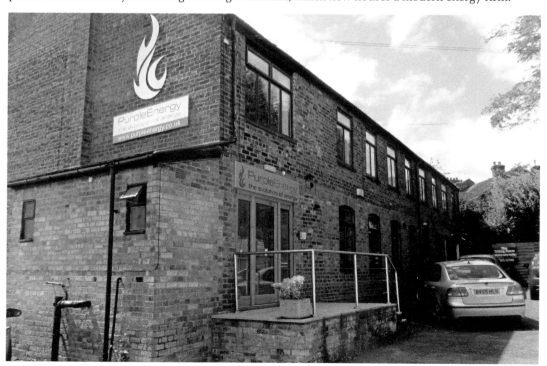

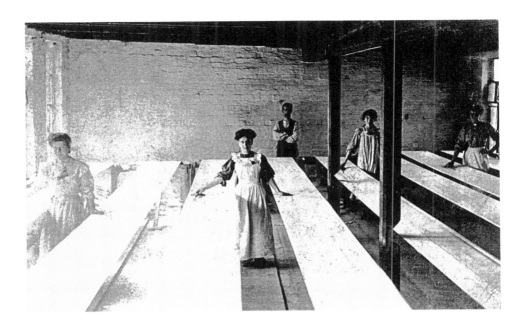

Textile Workers

The picture of 1915 shows women at work in the fustian mill. Work meant running up and down the lengths of cotton, cutting the threads as required. It was immensely hard work. A former worker recalled working hours being 6 a.m. to 6 p.m., with two half-hour breaks, for weekly wages of around 10s (50p). A tough side-apron protected the clothes worn and wooden clogs protected the feet. 'It was slavery' was her final comment. (Philip Leese). The workers illustrated in the more modern and mechanised nylon factory certainly appear to have much improved conditions. G. H. Heath's factory was set up in Butt Lane after 1945 and, by 1954, employed over 300 workers. A contemporary report commented on a place where 'it was a pleasure to work'! The factory eventually closed in 1988 and the textile industry came to an end in Kidsgrove.

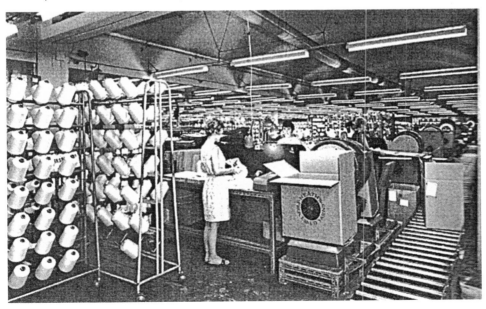

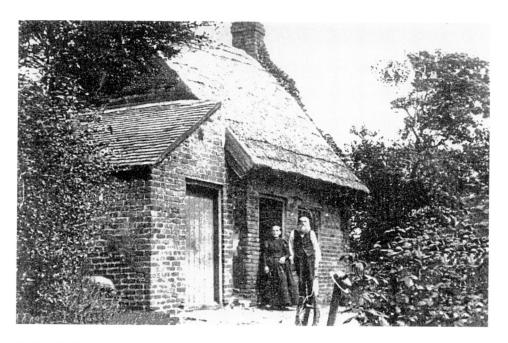

'A Bit of Old Butt Lane', Matthew and Louisa Sherratt

It seems likely that Old Butt Lane was the site of the early village of Butt Lane, though now it appears simply as a quiet backwater off the main Congleton Road. The thatched cottage, depicted in the very old photograph, has been entitled anonymously as 'a bit of Old Butt Lane'. It belonged to Matthew and Louisa Sheratt and has now gone. Parts of the lane, however, still retain a quiet, rural air as the cottage and its setting amply show in the recent picture.

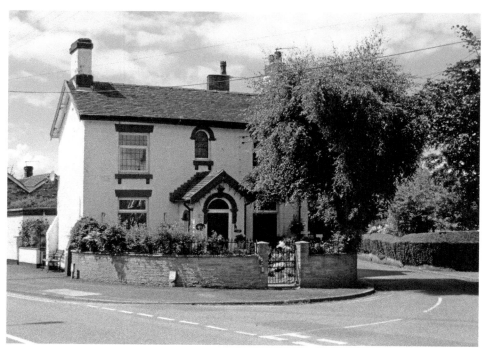

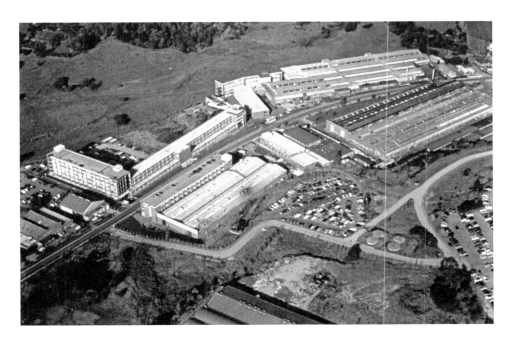

The Nelson Industrial Estate

Many of the old industries in the Kidsgrove area had collapsed in the interwar period, causing unemployment. As the Second World War approached its end, the Kidsgrove town council decided to set up an industrial estate. The Nelson Industrial Estate, one of the first in the country, was the result. The biggest success was the attraction of English Electric to the site. Starting with around 200 employees, the company expanded and went through a series of mergers, becoming English Electric-ICL and GEC-Elliot Automation with a working force of over 4,000. The size of the operation is indicated by the aerial photograph. By the early years of this century, these large firms had gone. However, the site is still used by a diverse range of firms, one of which is illustrated in the recent picture.

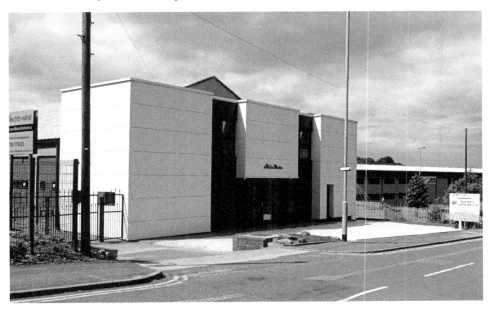

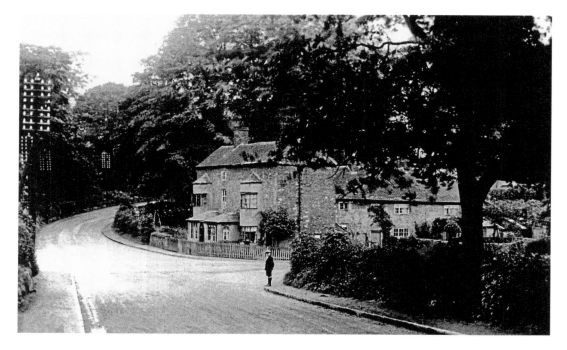

Red Bull Crossroads

As the recent photograph shows, this is a very busy junction where the A34 crosses the A50. In a quieter age a picture could be taken of the crossroads with no traffic and one young bystander. There is still housing around the crossroads but now hidden by trees. The once well-known landmark here, shown in the old photograph, is the impressive three-storey house on the corner, later demolished.

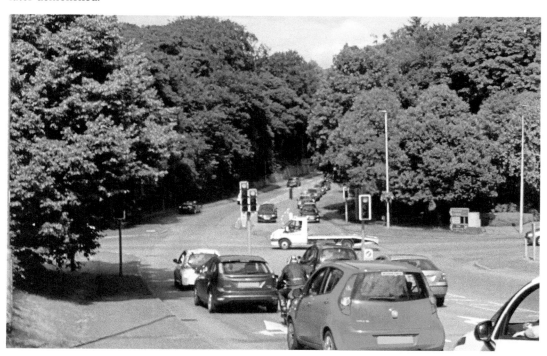

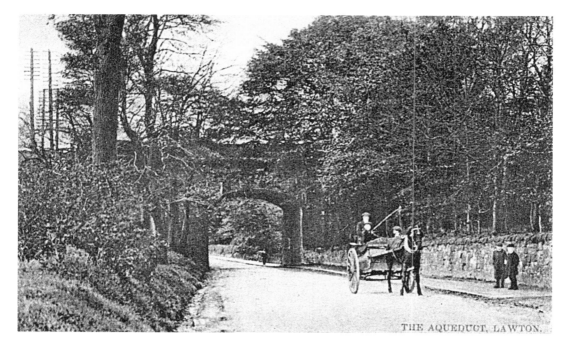

THE AQUEDUCT, LAWTON.

Macclesfield Canal Aqueduct, Liverpool Road

As Liverpool Road approaches Red Bull crossroads, it runs under the aqueduct of Telford's Macclesfield Canal. That canal, having run parallel with the Trent Mersey from Hardingswood, swings north and crosses the road at this point. The old picture again shows a slower pace of life in the early twentieth century. Now the road is busy and a car business occupies the ground on the left. The journey ends here as a roadside sign indicates entry back into Kidsgrove.

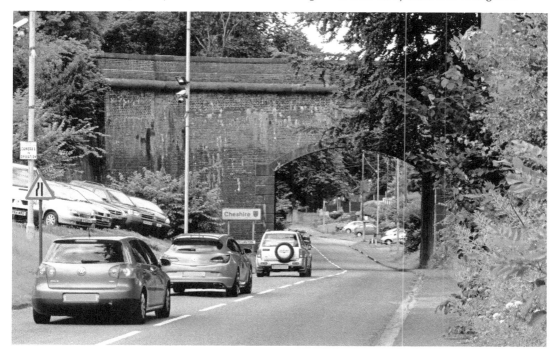

Acknowledgements

As I travelled around Butt Lane and Kidsgrove, seeking historical sites and background, everyone I met said 'have you talked to Philip Leese?' Fortunately I had and I cannot over emphasise my debt to him in writing this book. He freely and generously gave me his time and shared his great store of historical knowledge of the area with me. I must also thank the staff of Kidsgrove Library for all their help, as I constantly raided their wonderful collection of photographs and documents.

Many others gave me information and material for the book. These included: Jane Gould, Cllr Terry Turner, Cllr Reginald Bailey, Brenda Proctor, Jane Sheldon, M.Rigby, and Chris Brough.

Photographs:
The following people allowed me to use their historical photographs which enriched the book:

Allan S. Baker: the Birchenwood rail cutting (p. 9) and from his collection, the tunnel (p. 10)
Basil Jeuda: the Trent & Mersey canal (p.45) the Loop Line Station (p.30) Kidsgrove Station (p. 47)
David Fisher: Birchenwood Railway (p. 7), the electric tug photographs (p. 46), the railway tunnel (p. 65)
Jon Goodwin and Robin Witter: Inside the Brindley tunnel (pp. 42, 43.)

Linda Forrester has used all her computer skills to reduce a great mass of material into book form, and did it all with such patience. Jane has again revealed just how good a photographer she is and how patient she is with the trials and tribulations of book production. Then there is the support of Emma, Katie, Ruth, Sarah and Mick.

Useful books: Philip Leese, *Butt Lane, 1900-2000*; Philip Leese, *Kidsgrove As It Was*; also articles by Philip in the series, *Best of Kidsgrove Times*; R. Simmons, *Kidsgrove, Talke & Mow Cop*; Allan S. Baker, *The Potteries Loop Line*; Basil Jeuda, *The North Staffordshire Railway*.